Student
GUIDE
volume 2

PROGRAM AUTHOR
Timothy Shanahan, Ph.D.
Professor of Urban Education at the University of Illinois at Chicago
Director of the UIC Center for Literacy.

PEARSON READING INTERVENTION ADVISORY BOARD

Donald Deshler, Ph.D.
Professor of Education and Special Education, University of Kansas

Cynthia Greenleaf, Ph.D.
Co-Director of Strategic Literacy Initiative, WestEd, Oakland, California

John Guthrie, Ph.D.
Professor of Human Development, University of Maryland at College Park

Ernest Morrell, Ph.D.
Assistant Professor of Teacher Education, Michigan State University

GLOBE FEARON
Pearson Learning Group

REVIEWERS

We thank the following educators who provided valuable comments and suggestions during the development of the Student Guides:

Debi Glanton, Conyers, GA; Karen S. McDaniels, Miami, FL; Irene G. Mortensen, Quakertown, NJ; Yvonne E. Paranick, Oil City, PA; Sr. Mary Jean Raymond, Cleveland, OH; Maria Schneider, Ft. Myers, FL; Vickie L. Scraper, Wichita, KS; Dr. Margaret M. Smith, Las Vegas, NV

PROJECT STAFF

Art and Design: Tricia Battipede, Evelyn Bauer, Sharon Bozek, Bernadette Hruby, Salita Mehta, Elizabeth Nemeth, Alison O'Brien, April Okano, Angel Weyant

Editorial: Laura Axler, Leslie Feierstone Barna, Brian Hawkes, Cindy Kane, Madeline Boskey Olsen, Patricia Peters, Jennie Rakos, Emily Shenk, Constance Shrier, Maury Solomon, Tara Walters, Shirley White

Inventory: Jean Wohlgemuth

Marketing: Ken Clinton, Andrea Spaeth

Production/Manufacturing: Irene Belinsky, Laura Benford-Sullivan, Carlos Blas, Mark Cirillo, Jeff Engel, Leslie Greenberg, Ruth Leine, Susan Levine, Karyn Mueller

Publishing Operations: Richetta Lobban, Kate Matracia, Debi Schlott

PHOTO AND ILLUSTRATION CREDITS

All photography © Pearson Education, Inc. (PEI) unless otherwise specifically noted.

Cover: *r.* © Rykoff Collection/Corbis. 1: *m.* Jack Hollingsworth/Photodisc/Getty Images, Inc. 5: © Bettmann/Corbis. 6: David R. Frazier/Photo Researchers, Inc. 18: © Jim Reed/Corbis. 24: Jorn Georg Tomter/Getty Images, Inc. 27: *t.* Dave King/DK Images; *b.* Dave King/DK Images. 33: Erich Lessing/Art Resource, NY. 39: Kevin Summers/Getty Images, Inc. 42: AP/Wide World Photo. 48: © Areo Graphics, Inc./Corbis. 54: Eric Pearle/Getty Images, Inc. 56: *t.r.* Robert Sullivan/AFP/Getty Images, Inc.; *b.r.* PhotoDisc, Inc. 57: *t.* Jack Hollingsworth/Photodisc/Getty Images, Inc. 80: AP/Wide World Photo. 83: © Corbis. 95: Kirby, Smith &Wilkins/Roadside America. 98: Rafael Macia/Photo Researchers, Inc. 109: © RoadsideAmerica.com. 110: © Annie Griffiths Belt/Corbis. 112: *t.r.* AP/Wide World Photo; *b.r.* PhotoDisc, Inc. 113: *t.l.* © Rykoff Collection/Corbis; *t.r.* Jack Hollingsworth/Photodisc/Getty Images, Inc. 118: AP/Wide World Photo. 124: © Araldo de Luca/Corbis. 130: © Carol Cohen/Corbis. 136: © Ric Ergenbright/Corbis. 145: John Lepine © Science Museum, London/DK Images. 151: © Bettmann/Corbis. 154: D.E. Cox Photo Library ChinaStock. 160: © Roger Ressmeyer/Corbis. 166: Andrew McKinney © DK Images. 168: *t.r.* © Kimberly White/Corbis; *b.r.* PhotoDisc, Inc.;. 169: *t.* bkgd. Jack Hollingsworth/Photodisc/Getty Images, Inc.; *t.l.* Thais Baldin; *t.m.* Rudy Garcia-Tolson; *t.r.* Lucretia Birdinground; *m.l.* Tyrel Bernadini; *m.r.* Keisha McDaniel. 186: © Myrleen Ferguson Cafe/PhotoEdit. 192: Brian Caldwell. 195: © Bettmann/Corbis. 201: *t.* David Murray/DK Images; *b.* Ian O'Leary/DK Images. 210: Peter Buckley/Prentice Hall, High School. 216: *bkgd.* Russ Lappa/Prentice Hall School; inset © Hulton-Deutsch/Corbis. 222: Nick Koudis/Getty Images, Inc. 224: *t.r.* © Gianni Dagli Orti/Corbis; *b.r.* PhotoDisc, Inc.

Illustrations: Cover: *t.l.* Keith Robinson; *b.l.* Jamel Akib. All coach characters on vocabulary "Your Turn" pages: KATMO. 1: Jamel Akib. 12: Matt Vincent. 57: Keith Robinson. 61, 62, 68: Craig Phillips. 74: Glin Dibley. 88: James Elston. 89: Tyrone McCarthy. 104: Dusty Deyo. 117: Matt Vincent. 123: Shane Evans. 138: Ben Shannon. 139: Paul Mirocha. 180: Dan Trush. 207: XNR Productions, Inc.

ISBN: 0-13-024777-4

Printed in the United States of America

11 12 13 14 15 V0UD 19 18 17 16 15

Globe Fearon
Pearson Learning Group

1-800-321-3106
www.pearsonlearning.com

CONTENTS

UNIT 4

Staying Alive

Read on Your Own 4, 7, 10, 13, 16, 19, 22, 25, 28, 31, 34, 37, 40, 43, 46, 49, 52, 55

Fluency
Match expression to content, 6, 33, 42. Use punctuation marks as clues to expression and phrasing, 12, 39, 54. Do a practice read for smoother reading, 18, 24, 27. Use a conversational tone and pace, 48.

UNIT 5

Strange Journeys

Fluency
Use punctuation as cues to expression and phrasing, 62, 89. Read every word, 68. Match expression to the author's tone, 74. Match expression to the content, 80. Identify and practice reading difficult words, 95. Keep up pace to maintain interest, 98. Read first for understanding, then for phrasing, 104. Vary your expression, 83, 110.

UNIT 6

Nature in the Extreme

INFERENCING

Fluency
For smoothness, practice pausing at punctuation and breaks in text, 118, 124, 136. Vary the volume, 130. Practice reading with accuracy, 139. Change tone and expression to reflect content, 145, 160. Read as if you were conversing, 151, 166. Look up unfamiliar words in a dictionary, 154.

UNIT 7

Success Stories

Fluency
Use punctuation marks as clues to correct phrasing, 174. Practice reading difficult or boldfaced words ahead of time, 180, 195. Pause before and after subheads, 186. Pause at natural breaks between phrases, 192. Vary expression, 201. Keep up pace to maintain interest, 207. Use expression to highlight interesting points, 210. Read in a relaxed pace, 216. Pause and use pacing to show transition between segments, 222.

Staying ALIVE

COMPREHENSION
LEARN TO RECOGNIZE THE DIFFERENT WAYS TEXT CAN BE STRUCTURED

INDEPENDENT READING
Staying Alive
Includes "Lost! The Roanoke Adventure" and "How to Survive"

VOCABULARY

WORDS:
Know them!
Use them!
Learn all about them!

FLUENCY
Make your reading smooth and accurate, one tip at a time.

Make Words Yours!

Learn the WORDS

Below are some words you will be reading in the next two weeks. These are words you will often see in your textbooks and other reading.

WORD AND EXPLANATION	EXAMPLE	WRITE AN EXAMPLE
Findings are what you learn or discover from doing an investigation or research.	Scientists often lecture about their **findings**.	What kinds of historical **findings** have you learned about?
When you **guarantee** something, you promise that it will be done.	We can **guarantee** that the Sun will rise tomorrow.	What can you **guarantee** a friend?
Something is **mutual** if you have the same feelings about it as someone else does.	A club includes people with a **mutual** interest or hobby.	What **mutual** interests do you and your friends have?
A **plea** is a strong request for help.	Many people always answer a Red Cross **plea** for blood donors.	When is a time you answered someone's **plea** for help?
If you **rebel**, you resist authority or something that tries to control you.	The American colonists **rebelled** against Great Britain.	What are some reasons that groups of people **rebel**?
To **seclude** is to remove or separate from others. Something that is **secluded** is in a place by itself.	Doctors sometimes **seclude** sick people.	When do you feel like **secluding** yourself?
Sincere means honest or genuine.	Give a **sincere** answer to a serious question.	Who is the most **sincere** person you know?
To **submit** is to give in or to give something over to someone else.	A well-trained dog will **submit** to many commands.	What steps would you take to **submit** a job application?

→YOUR TURN

Answer these questions and be ready to explain your answers.

1. Could you *submit* a project after the due date? _____

2. Can a comment be *sincere* if you are laughing when you say it? _____

3. Would you *rebel* if your school cut back the sports and music programs? _____

4. Did you ever *seclude* yourself for a day? _____

Choose the right word

> findings guarantee mutual plea
> rebel seclude sincere submit

Fill each blank with the correct word.

5. The two sides bargained until they finally came to a _____ agreement.

6. The reporters could not _____ that the _____ were true.

7. We sent out an urgent _____ for help as the fire began to spread.

8. Many writers like to work alone and _____ themselves for days.

9. I would not _____ to my opponent.

10. Was the coach _____ or just trying to make us feel better?

11. At times, people will _____ against an unjust law.

> You will be reading about an early American colony. What if you started a colony in a strange new place?

Show that you know

Answer the questions. Use sentences.

12. What *findings* about the place would you want to know before you went?

13. What kind of *plea* would you make for people to help you start a colony?

14. Why would it be important for the people who go with you to have *mutual* goals?

15. How would you try to *guarantee* that you would be safe in the new place?

READ on your OWN
Staying Alive, pages 3–7

BEFORE YOU READ

What do you think it would be like to get on a ship and travel across an ocean to start a new life?

AS YOU READ

Preview pages 3–7 of "Lost! The Roanoke Adventure." (STOP)
What do the pictures on the pages tell you about the chapter?
What does the chapter title tell you about the chapter?

_____

_____

_____

_____

_____

Now read pages 3–7 of "Lost! The Roanoke Adventure." (STOP)
How did previewing the pictures and the title of the chapter help you understand what you read?

_____

_____

_____

VOCABULARY
Watch for the words you are learning about.

mutual: shared

findings: things that are learned

rebel: go against

FLUENCY
Pay attention to punctuation as you read aloud.

AFTER YOU READ

What do you think was the most exciting part of the pages you just read? Explain why it was exciting.

TEXT STRUCTURE: Previewing to Identify Text Structure

How to Use Text Structure

Preview text to get an idea of its organization and purpose.

Identify the text structure. Use clues and signal words to identify problem and solution, description, sequence, cause and effect, and compare and contrast.

In some writing, you will have to **identify multiple structures** in text.

Summarize text by thinking about its structure.

Learn the STRATEGY

All writing is organized or structured in a way that serves a particular purpose. In this unit, you will learn about each of the text structures listed on the right. You'll also learn how to identify each one while you are reading.

Good readers preview what they intend to read in order to learn about the structure and purpose of the text. Before reading a text word for word, preview it by reading the title and subtitles. Then read the opening and closing sentences or paragraphs. Also look at any pictures and diagrams.

The text structure of the passage below is description. You will learn more about this text structure later in this unit. For now, preview the passage by looking at the picture and reading the caption and first sentence. Then read the entire passage before answering the question in the side column.

TEXT STRUCTURES
• Problem and Solution
• Description
• Sequence of Events
• Compare and Contrast
• Cause and Effect

Sometimes, I think about Blackhawk, the Native American guide. Blackhawk led us to our new home in the wilderness. He knew the route and its dangers like the back of his hand. He spoke the languages of the many Native American groups we met. He taught us how to deal with the harsh winter snows and the constant demands on our energy. Without his help, I'm sure we would have died along the way.

A Native American guide

What were you able to tell about the passage by reading the first sentence, looking at the picture, and reading the caption?

_____
_____
_____
_____
_____
_____
_____

➤ YOUR TURN

Preview the descriptive passage "She Guided Them Westward." Then read the passage and answer the questions below.

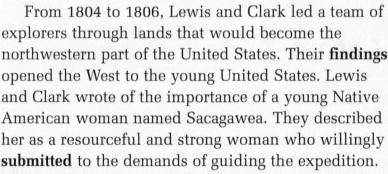

She Guided Them Westward

Sacagawea, the
Native American guide

....
1. What could you tell about the passage by reading the title?
....

....
2. What could you tell about the passage by looking at the picture and reading the caption?
....

From 1804 to 1806, Lewis and Clark led a team of explorers through lands that would become the northwestern part of the United States. Their **findings** opened the West to the young United States. Lewis and Clark wrote of the importance of a young Native American woman named Sacagawea. They described her as a resourceful and strong woman who willingly **submitted** to the demands of guiding the expedition.

The explorers started from St. Louis, Missouri. Sacagawea joined them in North Dakota. From 1805 to 1806, she traveled with them to Oregon and then back to Missouri. Lewis and Clark's praise for Sacagawea was **sincere**. She was an essential part of the expedition. She led it through hostile territory and helped obtain food for its members. She served as an interpreter in discussions with Native American groups, who answered the explorers' **pleas** for horses. She did all this while taking care of her infant son. The baby's presence on the journey showed the Native American groups that the expedition was peaceful.

Change the expression in your voice to show whether information is surprising, serious, or descriptive.

FLUENCY

READ on your OWN
Staying Alive, pages 8–10

BEFORE YOU READ

Think about the last pages you read in "Lost! The Roanoke Adventure." What happened to the Roanoke colonists?

AS YOU READ

Preview and then read "David, 1587," pages 8–10.
Then complete the chart below.

VOCABULARY
Watch for the words you are learning about.

submit: to give in or give something over to someone else

guarantee: to promise with great confidence

rebelling: resisting against something

FLUENCY
Watch for quotation marks that indicate dialogue. Read dialogue in a way that shows how the characters are feeling.

What I learned from the first paragraph	What I learned from the last paragraph	What I learned about how the chapter begins and ends

AFTER YOU READ

How do you think you would feel if you were traveling to a place that no one you knew had ever visited?

Get Wordwise!
Latin Word Origins

Learn More About the WORDS

Knowing a **word's origin** can help you remember the meaning of the word. Below are some words you have studied. Each word comes from the ancient language of Latin and is still closely related in meaning to the Latin meaning.

WORD AND LATIN ORIGIN	EXPLANATION	DRAW A CONCLUSION
Mutual comes from **mutuus**, meaning lent or borrowed.	**Mutual** means having the same feelings about something.	What is **mutual** about lending or borrowing?
Plea comes from **plaecere**, meaning to please or something to be decided.	A **plea** is a strong request for help.	When you make a **plea**, is something still to be decided? Explain.
Rebel comes from **rebellis**, which is from **re-** + **bellum**, meaning war. **Rebellis** means fight back.	To **rebel** means to resist authority.	Does a person who **rebels** fight back? Explain.
Seclude comes from **secludere**, meaning separate.	To **seclude** means to separate from others.	If you are **secluded**, what might you be separated from?
Sincere comes from **sincerus**, which means whole, pure, or genuine.	**Sincere** means honest or genuine.	How does being pure and genuine relate to being **sincere**?

→YOUR TURN

Answer these questions and be ready to explain your answers.

1. Can a *sincere* speech move an audience to tears? _____

2. Must players come to a *mutual* decision about the rules before they play a game? _____

3. Should you answer every *plea* you hear? _____

4. Is a *secluded* place a good place to study? _____

5. Is breaking a rule the same as *rebelling*? _____

Choose the right word

:···:
: mutual   seclude   rebel   sincere   plea :
:···:

Fill each blank with the correct word. You will use some words twice.

6. The arguing teams finally came to a
   [_____] agreement.

7. The fans' [_____] for the band to play another song was answered.

8. Did the students [_____] against the suggestion that no one should bring a backpack to class?

9. When I feel upset, I [_____] myself in a quiet part of my backyard.

10. Raul was so [_____] that no one ever questioned his honesty.

11. The teacher answered my
    [_____] for help with the test question.

12. Tara likes to [_____] herself in the quiet garden.

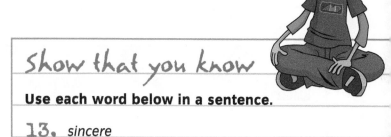

Think about what you have read in this unit so far. Then write about some things you have learned.

Show that you know

Use each word below in a sentence.

13. *sincere*
_____
_____
_____
_____
_____
_____

14. *rebel*
_____
_____
_____
_____
_____
_____
_____

READ on your OWN
Staying Alive, pages 11–13

BEFORE YOU READ

Think about the last pages you read in "Lost! The Roanoke Adventure." Where was the ship called the *Lion* sailing to?

AS YOU READ

Preview and read "On Roanoke Island," pages 11–13.
Fill in the chart below.

What I learned from the first paragraph	What I learned from the last paragraph	What I learned about how the chapter begins and ends

VOCABULARY
Watch for the words you are learning about.

secluded: separated and far from anything

submit: to give to someone

plea: request

seclude: to separate

FLUENCY
Preview text before you read aloud. You can practice reading words that are hard to pronounce.

AFTER YOU READ

What was the most interesting part of the chapter you just read? Explain why it was interesting to you.

TEXT STRUCTURE: Problem/Solution in Narrative Writing

How to Use Text Structure

Preview text to get an idea of its organization and purpose.

Identify the text structure. Use clues and signal words to identify problem and solution, description, sequence, cause and effect, and compare and contrast.

In some writing, you will have to **identify multiple structures** in text.

Summarize text by thinking about its structure.

Learn the STRATEGY

Narrative writing can tell a story about real characters and events or about made-up or fictional characters and events. The story may describe a problem that a character has. By the end of the story, the character has often solved the problem. The term *problem and solution* is used to describe the structure of a story that involves a problem and solution.

Good readers try to determine if a story has a problem-and-solution text structure. They do this by looking for descriptions of problems and solutions in the text. Identifying text structure, such as problem and solution, can help readers remember what they have read.

Read the passage below. Then complete the exercises in the side column.

Maya wanted desperately to go on the class camping trip, but something huge stood in her way. She was afraid of the great outdoors! To Maya, cities were safe and secure, but nature was dangerous and unpredictable. Every tree looked like a grizzly bear, and every rock hid a poisonous snake. Then Maya had a great idea. She would visit the meadow and the little grove of trees in the city park every day from now until the day of the trip. While in those familiar places, she would imagine she was in the wilderness and enjoying it. When the day of the trip finally came, the wilderness wouldn't seem so wild after all!

Underline the problem and the solution in the passage.

Circle the best description of the problem below.

a. Maya doesn't feel safe in cities.
b. Maya thinks camping is boring.
c. Maya is afraid of the outdoors.

Circle the best description of the solution below.

a. Maya decides not to go on the trip.
b. Maya visits a city park to get used to the outdoors.
c. Maya decides to just ignore her fears and go on the trip.

► YOUR TURN

Read "An Agreement." Then complete the exercise below.

1. Describe the problem and solution in the chart below.

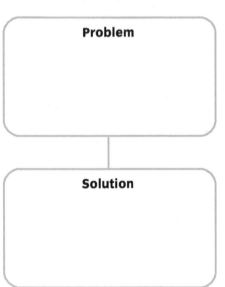

Problem

Solution

AN AGREEMENT

It was the first spring hike for the Highland Hikers group. Jeffrey was the least popular member of the group, probably because he was something of a **rebel**. He knew a lot about following trails, but he was more interested in spotting wildlife than in hiking. He often complained about the difficult hikes, while the other hikers complained about his slowness.

That Saturday, Jeffrey was lagging behind as usual. Suddenly, he saw something moving. In a **secluded** spot away from the trail, a deer was grazing. Jeffrey stopped to watch it. When he looked for the other hikers, he realized they were far ahead. When he finally caught up with them, he could tell they were angry with him, but they also looked scared.

"We think we are following the wrong trail and it's getting dark," one hiker explained. No one wanted to spend the night lost on the mountain. They hoped Jeffrey could help.

Jeffrey looked at a trail map and then checked the sun setting in the west. He pointed out that the trail they were on went north but that there was another trail just ahead that went east. "We need to hike east to reach our camp," Jeffrey said.

They were back in camp by nightfall. After dinner, Jeffrey and the rest of the Highland Hikers reached a **mutual** agreement. He promised he wouldn't complain while hiking, and they **guaranteed** that they would allow him time to look for animals along the way.

2. How did identifying the problem and solution help you understand the passage?

Use commas and periods as guides for when to pause while reading.

FLUENCY

READ on your OWN
Staying Alive, pages 14–16

BEFORE YOU READ

Think about the last pages you read in "Lost! The Roanoke Adventure." How did David and Wanchese agree to help each other?

AS YOU READ

Read "Farewell to John White," pages 14–16.
In the chart below, describe the problem the colonists face and the solution proposed by Ananias Dare.

VOCABULARY
Watch for the words you are learning about.

pleas: strong requests for help or to be heard

findings: results of some kind of investigation

sincerely: in a genuine way

guarantee: to promise with great confidence

sincere: honest or genuine

FLUENCY
Pay attention to punctuation. Remember to pause when you see a comma and stop briefly at a period.

The Problem

The Solution

AFTER YOU READ

Choose the most interesting character or event in this chapter. Describe the character or event.

Make Words Yours!

Learn the WORDS

As you read more, you'll come across these words. This is your chance to get to know them better.

WORD AND EXPLANATION	EXAMPLE	WRITE AN EXAMPLE
If someone is your **ancestor**, you are descended from that person. Grandparents and great-grandparents are **ancestors**.	Some people in the United States have an **ancestor** who was here before European explorers came.	In which part of the world did your **ancestors** live?
The **bulk** of something is the biggest part of it.	The **bulk** of an iceberg is beneath the water.	What do you do with the **bulk** of your time?
Something that has **clarity** is clear or easy to understand.	The instructions were given with such **clarity** that everyone understood them.	What happens when your plans with friends don't have **clarity**?
Your **heritage** is the traditions that have been handed down from past generations.	Our right to vote is part of the American **heritage**.	What traditions from your **heritage** do you celebrate?
The **latter** is the second of two things.	If I had to choose between sleet and rain, I'd choose the **latter**.	Which is the **latter** of your first two classes each day?
When people or things **prosper**, they do well, especially in earning money.	Very few people **prosper** in their jobs without working hard.	How do salespeople help a company to **prosper**?
To **relate** is to be connected or to make a connection. You can **relate** to how someone feels.	It can be hard to **relate** to people who lived during colonial times.	What is something you've read recently that **relates** to your life?
To **taper** is to become gradually narrower toward one end or to gradually lessen.	The bottom of an ice-cream cone **tapers**.	Why does a screwdriver **taper** at the end?

YOUR TURN

Yes or No?

Answer these questions and be ready to explain your answers.

1. Could a person's *ancestors* still be alive? _____

2. Is the *latter* item in a pair the first item? _____

3. Would the *clarity* of a lake tempt you to go swimming? _____

4. Do pencils *taper* at the end? _____

Write about adventures to show that you know the words.

Choose the right word

> ancestor   bulk   clarity   heritage
> latter   prosper   relate   taper

Fill each blank with the correct word.

5. The candles [ ] at the top.

6. It was difficult for the colonists to [ ] at first.

7. Scientists try to [ ] new discoveries to what they already know.

8. Domestic dogs all have the wolf as a common [ ].

9. Tom's grandfather is proud of his Native American [ ].

10. I rode the go-carts and the Ferris wheel, but the [ ] was my favorite.

11. To make your point, you must explain your position with [ ].

12. During the winter, the [ ] of the colonists' food was dried meats.

Show that you know

Answer the questions. Use sentences.

13. What kind of adventure would *relate* to your interests?

14. How could you *prosper* from an adventure?

15. How would you spend the *bulk* of your time on your adventure?

16. How could finding out about your *heritage* be an adventure?

READ on your OWN
Staying Alive, pages 17–19

BEFORE YOU READ

Think about the last pages you read in "Lost! The Roanoke Adventure." What kinds of things did David do to help the other colonists?

AS YOU READ

Read "Hungry," pages 17–19. (STOP)
In the chart below, describe the problem the colonists face and the solution David proposes.

The Problem

The Solution

VOCABULARY
Watch for the words you are learning about.

latter: second of two things

relate: to tell about

prosper: to live well

rebel: to go against

pleading: begging

FLUENCY
Read in a relaxed way, as if you were talking to a friend.

AFTER YOU READ

Have you ever had an idea that you felt was right, but then had to convince other people to agree to your idea? What happened?

TEXT STRUCTURE: Problem/Solution in Expository Writing

How to Use Text Structure

Preview text to get an idea of its organization and purpose.

Identify the text structure. Use clues and signal words to identify problem and solution, description, sequence, cause and effect, and compare and contrast.

In some writing, you will have to **identify multiple structures** in text.

Summarize text by thinking about its structure.

Learn the STRATEGY

In expository writing, authors explain something to their readers. Authors often describe a problem and ways in which the problem can be solved. Take, for example, a passage that explains how to prepare for a long hiking trip. The author could describe the problem of carrying enough food for several days. Then the author could explain ways in which hikers solve this problem.

Identifying the problem and solution while reading a piece of expository writing will help you understand and recall what you read. The following signal words and phrases can indicate that an expository passage has a problem and solution structure: *if/then, therefore, the problem is, the question is, one possible solution,* and *one proposal is.* Read the passage below. Then complete the exercises in the side column.

A hurricane heading for a populated area is a major problem. It can cause deadly injuries and widespread property damage. Fortunately, hurricanes can be forecast well in advance. People can be alerted before hurricanes strike. One possible solution to the problem of an approaching hurricane is to order an evacuation. Unfortunately, an evacuation can cause traffic jams as everyone tries to leave the area at once. Another solution is to open emergency shelters in gymnasiums and auditoriums. Emergency shelters can house a lot of people in one place. The authorities can use their resources more efficiently. They don't have to take care of people who are spread out all over.

In the passage, circle the problem that is described. Then underline the solutions.

How did identifying the problem and solutions in the paragraph help you to better understand it? Circle a letter below to indicate your answer.

a. It helped me understand that hurricanes are always major disasters.

b. It helped me understand how each solution could help prevent or lessen problems caused by a hurricane.

c. It helped me understand that evacuation is the only good solution to the problem of a hurricane.

YOUR TURN

Read "Hurricanes Hit Farms, Too." Then complete the problem-and-solution chart.

Hurricanes Hit Farms, Too

Hurricane Francis hit many farms in Florida. Farmers are in an especially difficult position when it comes to hurricane preparation. They can evacuate the area or move into emergency shelters. They can't take their farm animals and **bulky** farming equipment with them, though. All farmers, even **prosperous** ones, depend on their farms for income. They are likely to be very anxious to find a way to protect them. How do farmers solve the problem of protecting the people, animals, and equipment on their farms?

One option farmers have is to put the animals in the barn and make it as secure as possible. They may tie their equipment down, make sure the animals have food, and hope for the best. Even if farm equipment gets blown around, the farmers may be able to salvage it.

Farmers and their families may decide to remain on the farm in a fairly secure place. For example, they may ride out the hurricane in a storm cellar. They may decide to go to a nearby shelter, however. If they choose the **latter** option, they may be relieved to be in a safer place. They are likely to be very anxious about their untended farms, though.

Farmers may have a lot of cleanup to do after a hurricane. Fortunately, they often have lots of good neighbors who will lend a hand. In the country, neighbors often feel **related** to one another. They help each other out when emergencies occur.

Problem

Solution

Read the passage ahead of time to decide where to take breaths. This will help you read more smoothly.

FLUENCY

READ on your OWN
Staying Alive, pages 20–22

VOCABULARY
Watch for the words you are learning about

taper: to become increasingly smaller toward one end

bulk: the biggest part

tapered: coming to an end or a point

FLUENCY
Look for commas that signal the beginning and end of a phrase. You can pause after phrases to build excitement or to add emphasis.

BEFORE YOU READ

Think about the last pages you read in "Lost! The Roanoke Adventure." What did David think was the source of the colonists' problems?

AS YOU READ

Read "Poor Harvests," pages 20–22.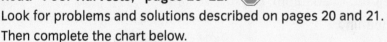
Look for problems and solutions described on pages 20 and 21.
Then complete the chart below.

The problems experienced by the colonists	The solution suggested by Wanchese

AFTER YOU READ

If you were worried about your food supply, how would you feel if someone like Wanchese arrived with food?

Get Wordwise!
Idioms

Learn More About the WORDS

Sometimes what we say isn't exactly what we mean.

"We're moving into a new apartment this weekend," Tyrone said.

"If you need help, I could lend a hand," Lee offered.

Think about Lee's offer to *lend a hand*. Do you think he will actually let Tyrone borrow his hand? No. This expression is called an **idiom**. *To lend a hand* means to be helpful. In an idiom, the words don't have their usual, or literal, meaning.

WORD	MEANING	RELATED IDIOM	USE THE IDIOM IN A SENTENCE
bulk	the biggest part	**The whole wad** means all of something.	It took the whole wad of money to
clarity	being clear or easy to understand	To **clear the air** means to get rid of negative emotions and differences.	We need to clear the air about
prosper	to do well, especially in earning money	If you **hit pay dirt**, you get a lot of money, often all at once.	The miner hit pay dirt and
relate	to be connected or make a connection	When you **see eye to eye** with someone, you totally agree with that person.	I try to see eye to eye
taper	to become increasingly narrower or less	To **dry up** is to gradually disappear.	My energy dries up
heritage	something handed down from past generations	When something is **in the genes**, it's a skill or characteristic that has been passed down through the generations.	It is in my genes to

▶YOUR TURN

Yes or No?

Answer these questions and be ready to explain your answers.

1. Is it easy to *relate* to someone who goes to a different school? _____

2. Will asking the right questions give you *clarity* about something? _____

3. Is the *bulk* of something just a small part of it? _____

4. Does the flame of a candle *taper* as it gets to the top? _____

5. Does someone with lots of friends *prosper*? _____

6. Can a person's *heritage* change? _____

Missing words

bulk   clarity   prosper   heritage   relate   taper

Fill each blank with the correct word.

7. Let's clear the air and get some _____ on what we're supposed to do.

8. It's hard to _____ to someone if you don't see eye to eye.

9. He used the _____ of his bank account when he spent the whole wad on a car.

10. My hope is to _____ by hitting pay dirt.

11. My energy begins to _____ off and dry up at the end of the day.

12. It's in my genes to assert my rights. I guess it comes from my American _____.

Show that you know some idioms by writing about adventure.

Show that you know

Use each idiom in a sentence.

13. *eye to eye*

14. *clear the air*

READ on your OWN
Staying Alive, pages 23–25

BEFORE YOU READ

Think about the pages you just read in "Lost! The Roanoke Adventure." What is the biggest problem that the colonists were facing on Roanoke?

VOCABULARY
Watch for the words you are learning about.

clarity: clearness

prosper: to live well

FLUENCY
Try to read in a relaxed way, as if you were talking to a friend.

AS YOU READ

Read "The Way of the Croatoans," pages 23–25.
Find the problem described in the first paragraph on page 23. Then look on page 25 for the solution that David proposes to the colonists. Then complete the chart below.

The problem	The solution David proposes

AFTER YOU READ

If you were one of the colonists and had to vote on the decision to move to the mainland with the Croatoans, how would you have voted? Explain why.

TEXT STRUCTURE: Description in Fiction and Nonfiction

How to Use Text Structure

Preview text to get an idea of its organization and purpose.

Identify the text structure. Use clues and signal words to identify problem and solution, description, sequence, cause and effect, and compare and contrast.

In some writing, you will have to **identify multiple structures** in text.

Summarize text by thinking about its structure.

Learn the STRATEGY

Writers often use description to create a picture in the reader's mind of a person, place, or thing. Descriptive writing helps the reader understand how someone or something looks, acts, works, feels, or thinks. Try to determine if a writer has used description to structure something that you are reading. You can do this by looking for words and phrases that signal that a story is descriptive. For example, suppose you read this sentence in a story.

The huge bolt of bright yellow fabric tumbled onto the dirty floor.

The words *huge, bright, yellow, tumbled,* and *dirty* are signal words. They indicate that you are reading descriptive writing.

Read the paragraph below. Then complete the exercises in the side column.

From the top of the mountain, I had been enjoying the splendid view of high peaks and deep valleys. Then I suddenly realized that the late-afternoon sun was fading quickly. I headed down the trail, anxious to get back to my camp before total darkness fell. After about a half hour of steady walking, I realized that the trail looked unfamiliar. Could I have taken the wrong trail down? Was I lost? I started racing down the mountain, stumbling over the gnarly roots in my path. My palms felt sweaty, and my breath was rapid and shallow. "Get a grip on yourself," I murmured in a shaky voice. "Instead of running blindly down the mountain, take out your compass and map, and figure out where you are."

Underline the words and phrases in the passage that signal that it is descriptive.

Look at the descriptive words and phrases in the last three sentences of the paragraph. How did they help you understand the paragraph?

_____
_____
_____
_____
_____

YOUR TURN

Read "Following in Their Footsteps." Then complete the exercises in the side column.

Following in Their Footsteps

1. List some of the signal words that indicate that the passage is descriptive.

2. How does knowing that description is the text structure of the passage help you understand it?

Stories of brave and daring wilderness guides are part of our national **heritage**. For generations, we've thrilled to old tales of wilderness guides. We've enjoyed hearing about how they forged paths over our nation's high peaks. Today, we thrill to similar stories of mountain guides. Mountains guides also lead climbers to the tops of towering mountains. The wilderness guide of the past is certainly the **ancestor** of today's mountain guide. Mountain guides possess many of the same abilities as the wilderness guide of old.

Mountain guides must be highly skilled in a wide range of outdoor activities. They must be skilled in mountaineering, rock climbing, and skiing. They must be strong, fit, and positive. They must also be brave and quick-witted. Extreme weather conditions are common on the **tapered** peaks of high mountains. Dangerous situations, such as violent storms, occur suddenly. Mountain guides need **clarity** of judgment to foresee danger. They also need training and experience to deal with unexpected emergencies.

Practice reading until you can read without mistakes. Then read the passage smoothly and at a pace that seems natural.

FLUENCY

READ on your OWN
Staying Alive, pages 26–28

BEFORE YOU READ

Think about the last pages you read in "Lost! The Roanoke Adventure." Why was David reluctant to present his point of view to the other colonists?

AS YOU READ

Read "A Vote," pages 26–28.
Reread the third and last paragraphs on page 27. In the chart below, list the descriptive words in each paragraph. Then explain how the descriptive words helped you understand the paragraph.

Descriptive words	How the descriptive words helped me understand the paragraph
Third paragraph	
Last paragraph	

VOCABULARY
Watch for the words you are learning.

ancestors: people from whom you are descended, such as great-grandparents

heritage: something you possess as a result of your situation or birth

bulky: large

FLUENCY
Reread a section a few times until you can read it smoothly.

AFTER YOU READ

Choose the most interesting thing you learned about a character in this chapter and tell what you learned.

TEXT STRUCTURE: Sequence

How to Use Text Structure

| **Preview text** to get an idea of its organization and purpose. | **Identify the text structure.** Use clues and signal words to identify problem and solution, description, sequence, cause and effect, and compare and contrast. | In some writing, you will have to **identify multiple structures** in text. | **Summarize text** by thinking about its structure. |

Learn the STRATEGY

Sequence means that details are presented in order from first to last. In writing, the structure of sequence can follow a series of events in time, or a series of steps that go from first to last. For example, instructions for making something are often written in sequence. Here are some signal words that indicate that an author has used sequence to structure a piece of writing: *first, then, next, once, before, later, afterward, when, finally,* and *eventually.* Graphic organizers can help to show a sequence. A timeline can be used to show a sequence of events and dates. A flowchart can be used to show a sequence of events or steps.

Read the passage below. Then complete the exercises in the side column.

Did you know that clams were an important food for some Native American groups who once lived near the seacoast? Clams are a good source of protein and are not difficult to find. In fact, finding enough clams for a pot of clam chowder doesn't take that long. Here's some advice for the beginner. First, gather your tools together. You'll need a shovel, pail, and some wooden sticks. Next, put on a pair of rubber wading boots and rubber gloves. Now you're ready for action. Once on the beach, start to look for the little holes that show a clam is below the sand. When you find a hole, mark it by pushing a stick into the sand. After you've marked as many spots as you need, start digging. You may have to dig down a foot or more to find each clam. Before long, however, you'll have a bucketful—enough for a delicious chowder!

Underline the signal words in the passage that indicate sequence.

Complete the flowchart for the steps described in the passage.

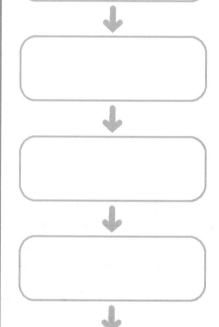

CLAMMING

Gather tools together.

↓

↓

↓

↓

Dig for clams.

Read "Early Native American Tools."
Then complete the exercises below.

Early Native American Tools

Thousands of years ago, the first North Americans arrived on this continent. Not much is known for certain about how they lived. At first, these early Native Americans were not great hunters. Over time, they developed more and more effective methods and tools, however. It was at this point that they began to **prosper**.

Their first hunting tools were crude. They were made of **tapered** sticks, heavy clubs, and stones. Then, the Native Americans started to use **tapered** sticks as spears. The point at the end of each spear was made of sharpened stone. Later, the Native Americans developed poisoned darts, traps, and weighted clubs. The people followed animal migrations. They limited their hunting to suit their needs.

Eventually, many Native Americans began to grow crops, such as corn. They used tools to dig in the earth. The methods and tools of the first North Americans are part of the **heritage** of Native Americans today.

Some early Native American tools

- -
1. Underline the words in the passage that signal sequence.
- -

2. Reread the second and third paragraphs. Complete the flowchart to show how Native American tools developed over time. The last box is done for you.

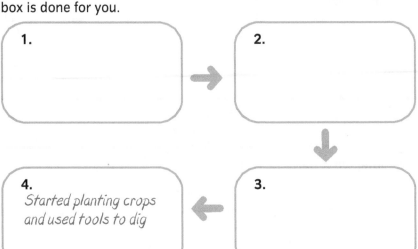

1.

2.

3.

4.
Started planting crops and used tools to dig

> **Practice reading difficult sentences in a passage. Then practice until you can read the entire passage without mistakes.**
>
> FLUENCY

READ on your OWN
Staying Alive, pages 29–31

VOCABULARY
Watch for the words you are learning about.

heritage: something you possess as a result of your situation or birth

ancestors: people from whom you are descended, such as great-grandparents

FLUENCY
Practice reading until you can read smoothly and accurately. Do not skip or substitute words.

BEFORE YOU READ

Think about the last pages you read in "Lost! The Roanoke Adventure." Why did David "feel like a Croatoan at heart"?

AS YOU READ

Read "New Ways," pages 29–31.
Reread the last three paragraphs on page 29. Think about the sequence of the events that are described. Then number each event listed in the chart to show the sequence of events from first to last.

Events in the last three paragraphs	Order of events
The children of the colonists began to marry the children of the Croatoans.	
Their new way of life began to feel familiar to the English colonists.	
David became a respected and skilled member of the band.	
The colonists began to dress as the Croatoans did.	

AFTER YOU READ

If you moved to a new place with new people, what parts of your heritage would you most want to keep?

Make Words Yours!

Learn the WORDS

Below are some words you will be reading in the next two weeks. These are words you will often see in your textbooks and other reading.

WORD AND EXPLANATION	EXAMPLE	WRITE AN EXAMPLE
If you have **awareness** of something, you know about it and keep it in mind.	Our **awareness** of the variety of life on Earth is always increasing.	How can you raise **awareness** for fire safety at your school?
Dependent means relying on someone or something for help.	A baby bird is completely **dependent** on its parents.	When are people **dependent** on others?
To **encounter** is to unexpectedly meet or come upon someone or something.	You'll **encounter** many new sights the first time you visit Yellowstone National Park.	How many people did you **encounter** on your way to school?
Nutritious foods make you healthy.	A sick person can get well faster by eating **nutritious** foods.	What are some **nutritious** snacks?
When you **retrieve** something, you get it and bring it back.	I taught my dog to **retrieve** a ball.	How would you **retrieve** a kite that is stuck in a tree?
Something is **scant** if there is barely enough of it.	The park had **scant** shelter, so some people got soaked in the rain.	If you were lost in the forest with a **scant** food supply, how would you survive?
When you have a **strategy** for doing something, you have a careful plan for getting it done.	Having a **strategy** in advance can save your life in a disaster.	What game requires a good **strategy** to win?
Torrential describes a rushing flow of water.	The **torrential** rains of a hurricane can cause widespread flooding.	What risk might a **torrential** rain cause near your home?

YOUR TURN

Answer these questions and be ready to explain your answers.

1. Is a can of soda *nutritious*? _____

2. Have you ever *encountered* a strange animal? _____

3. Does an ocean have a *scant* amount of water? _____

4. Is *strategy* important in football and chess? _____

Choose the right word

> awareness encounter torrential retrieve dependent nutritious strategy scant

Fill each blank with the correct word.

5. An [_____] of eating [_____] foods is important to our health.

6. I hope we don't [_____] a skunk during the hike.

7. Before we left, I ran back inside to [_____] my backpack.

8. Is offense or defense a better [_____] in a soccer match?

9. After the [_____] rains, there was [_____] evidence of footprints.

10. Your safety in a disaster may be [_____] on your preparation.

Show that you know the words by writing about natural disasters.

Show that you know

Complete the sentences.

11. In a flood, your family's safety could be *dependent* on _____

_____

_____

12. One way to raise *awareness* about dangerous storms is _____

_____

_____

13. *Torrential* rains can be dangerous because _____

_____

_____

14. After a flood I would try to *retrieve* _____

_____

_____

_____

_____

READ on your OWN
Staying Alive, pages 32–35

BEFORE YOU READ

Think about what it would be like to live through a disaster.
What kinds of things would you worry about?

AS YOU READ

Read pages 32–35 of "How to Survive."
Reread the second paragraph on page 32. Think about
the sequence of the events that are described. Then number
each event listed in the chart to show the sequence of the
events from first to last.

Events in the second paragraph	Order of events
The tornado knocks you down.	
The sky darkens.	
You see a tornado coming toward you.	
The air is calm.	

AFTER YOU READ

What was the most surprising thing you learned in the section you just
read? Tell somebody about what you found out.

VOCABULARY
Watch for the words you are
learning about.

encounter: to meet up with

strategy: plan

awareness: having knowledge
about

FLUENCY
When you see a question mark at
the end of a sentence, be sure to
make your voice rise slightly.

TEXT STRUCTURE: Identifying Fact and Opinion

How to Use Text Structure

Preview text to get an idea of its organization and purpose.	**Identify the text structure.** Use clues and signal words to identify problem and solution, description, sequence, cause and effect, and compare and contrast.	In some writing, you will have to **identify multiple structures** in text.	**Summarize text** by thinking about its structure.

Learn the STRATEGY

One way to help you understand and recall the points a writer is making is to look for facts and opinions. A fact can be proven. For example, read this statement: *Some of the world's largest volcanoes are found in Hawaii.* You could prove it if you looked up information about volcanoes. Now read this statement: *Volcanoes are the most interesting kind of natural disaster.* This is an opinion. It cannot be proved. Phrases such as *I think, I feel, I believe,* and *in my opinion* may signal that the writer is giving an opinion. Some writers use words such as *best* or *worst* to express their opinions.

As you read the passage, look for statements that are facts and opinions.

Some scientists study volcanoes. They pay attention to many things when a volcano is about to erupt. Small earthquakes in the area of a volcano are an early sign that it may erupt soon. Small earthquakes are caused by magma moving beneath the volcano. The volcano may vent steam and ash. That is really exciting. An important sign that a volcano is about to erupt is a sudden rise of lava beneath the surface, but the best part of volcano watching is when it is about to erupt. Studying volcanoes is a very interesting job!

Which statement is a **fact**?

a. Some scientists study volcanoes.

b. The best part of volcano watching is when it is about to erupt.

How can you tell that the statement you chose is a fact?

_____

_____

Which statement is an **opinion**?

a. The volcano may vent steam and ash.

b. Studying volcanoes is a very interesting job!

How can you tell that the statement you chose is an opinion?

_____

_____

Read "Whatever Happened to the Minoans?" and answer the questions.

Whatever Happened to the Minoans?

The island of Crete near Greece is the most beautiful island in Greece. Crete was once the home of the Minoans. The Minoan people lived well for almost 2,000 years. They were a peaceful people. Their artwork was the most beautiful of all early civilizations.

However, things changed. Scientists who study ancient people became **aware** that the Minoan people disappeared entirely! What happened to them? The nearby island of Thera was nearly destroyed by a powerful volcanic eruption between 2,000 and 3,500 years ago, which blew most of the island to pieces. That was amazing!

The eruption played a part in bringing about the end of the Minoan civilization. Even before the huge volcanic eruption on Thera, earthquakes had ruined several Minoan cities, leaving **scant** evidence of their civilization.

Scientists think the volcanic eruption on Thera caused huge waves to destroy some of Crete's cities. Earthquakes followed the eruption as well, and some scientists said the earthquakes were even more destructive than the volcanoes.

Scientists think that there was another cause of the Minoan peoples' downfall. It was the rise of another group of people—the Mycenaeans. The Mycenaeans were more warlike than the Minoans. The Myceneans attacked the Minoans. It seems that the natural disasters started the destruction and weakened the Minoan cities, but it took the Myceneans to totally destroy the Minoans.

1. Is this statement a fact or an opinion?
Crete was once the home of the Minoans.
   fact or **opinion**

How can you tell?

2. Is this statement a fact or an opinion?
Their artwork was the most beautiful of all early civilizations.
   fact or **opinion**

How can you tell?

3. Is this statement a fact or an opinion?
The Mycenaeans attacked the Minoans.
   fact or **opinion**

How can you tell?

Change the tone of your voice to show whether the text is surprising, serious, or descriptive.

FLUENCY

READ on your OWN
Staying Alive, pages 36–38

BEFORE YOU READ

Think about the pages you just read in "How to Survive."

Why is it important to be prepared for a disaster?

AS YOU READ

Read pages 36–38 of "How to Survive."

Complete the chart below, finding facts and opinions on the pages you just read.

Find this	What I found
Find a fact about earthquakes on page 36.	
Find a fact about the 1989 earthquake on page 38.	
Find a statement of the author's opinion on page 38.	

AFTER YOU READ

What was the most interesting thing you read in this section? Why did you find it interesting?

VOCABULARY

Watch for the words you are learning about.

nutritious: providing healthful food

dependent: relying on

FLUENCY

To maintain interest, read in a smooth, relaxed way, as if you were talking to someone you know.

Get Wordwise!
Prefixes Meaning "Not"

Learn More About the WORDS

A **prefix** is a word part that is added to the beginning of a word. A prefix changes the meaning of the word. Some prefixes make a word mean its opposite.

Possible means can be done. *Impossible* means cannot be done.

Visible means can be seen. *Invisible* means cannot be seen.

Prefixes that make a word mean its opposite are *un-*, *in-*, *im-*, and *ir-*.

WORD	EXAMPLE	ADD THE PREFIX	WRITE AN EXAMPLE
aware	I was suddenly **aware** that the house was shaking.	Add *un-* He was _____ that athletic shoes had to be worn on the gym floor.	When might you be **unaware** of your own birthday party?
dependent	As children grow older, they are no longer **dependent** on adults.	Add *in-* America became _____ in 1776.	What might it be like to be completely **independent**?
relate	Hurricanes and tornadoes are **related**; they are kinds of weather.	Add *un-* Earthquakes and tornadoes are _____ disasters.	What are two **unrelated** things?
retrievable	I tied a string to my model boat so it would be **retrievable** from the pond.	Add *ir-* I tried to remember the answer, but it was _____ .	What have you lost that was **irretrievable**?
sincere	Tasha sounded **sincere** when she said that she was sorry.	Add *in-* It is hard to trust an _____ person.	Why would a person make **insincere** comments?
movable	Most small items are **movable**.	Add *im-* A huge boulder is _____ .	What are some **immovable** objects around you?

YOUR TURN

Choose the right word

> independent irretrievable unrelated
> immovable insincere

Fill each blank with the correct word.

1. The rock was _____ so we planted the flowers around it.

2. The _____ store is not owned by a large company.

3. It's not nice to be _____ with others.

4. My book fell in the deep water, sank, and was _____.

5. The flood and the fire were _____, but they happened at the same time.

Which word works?

Circle the correct word in each pair.

6. Some metal objects are **retrievable / irretrievable** after a fire and can be used again.

7. I tried to catch the balloon as it floated away, but it was **retrievable / irretrievable**.

8. The kittens were completely **dependent / independent** on their mother for several days.

9. We decided to leave the group and create a(n) **dependent / independent** club.

10. A disaster emergency plan won't work if people are **aware / unaware** of it.

11. You should always be **aware / unaware** of the exits in any public building.

12. The words *ancestor* and *heritage* are **related / unrelated**.

> Show that you know the prefixes by answering questions about emergency situations.

Show that you know

Answer the questions. Use sentences.

13. What are the dangers of being with an *insincere* person during an emergency situation?

14. During a strong wind, what *immovable* object could you hold on to?

READ on your OWN
Staying Alive, pages 39–41

BEFORE YOU READ

Think about the last pages you read in "How to Survive."
Why is it important to make plans before a real disaster strikes?

AS YOU READ

Read pages 39–41 of "How to Survive."
Complete the chart below, finding facts and opinions on the pages
you just read.

Find this	What I found
Find a fact about the tornado's speed on page 39.	
Find a statement of the author's opinion about what a tornado sounds like on page 40.	
Find a fact about what happens before a tornado strikes on page 41.	

VOCABULARY
Watch for the words you are
learning about.

encounter: to meet up with

torrential: falling or flowing heavily

FLUENCY
Keep your tone relaxed, as if you
were talking to a friend.

AFTER YOU READ

Have you ever been in a situation that was a disaster or an emergency? What happened?

TEXT STRUCTURE: Compare and Contrast

How to Use Text Structure

Preview text to get an idea of its organization and purpose.

Identify the text structure. Use clues and signal words to identify problem and solution, description, sequence, cause and effect, and compare and contrast.

In some writing, you will have to **identify multiple structures** in text.

Summarize text by thinking about its structure.

Learn the STRATEGY

You have been learning about the ways that writers organize their ideas. Good readers look for clues to identify the structure of the text they read. One way writers organize text is to compare and contrast two things. Good readers know that thinking about comparisons and contrasts can help them as they read. It can help them notice details in text. It adds to their understanding and helps them remember what they read.

Comparing things means showing how they are alike. Clue words such as *like, same, similarly,* and *both* are signals that two things are being compared. Words such as *different, however, unlike, instead,* and *but* signal that things are being contrasted.

As you read the passage below look for comparisons and contrasts.

When you go hiking, no matter what season it is, wear the right clothes. In both summer and winter, dressing in layers is a good idea. You can always add or subtract layers to stay comfortable. If you are hiking in the winter, wear gloves or mittens to keep your hands warm. It is different in the summer. Then you want to stay cool, so try to dress lighter.

You should always cover your ears in the winter because it is no fun to have ears that are cold. It hurts! On the other hand, on a hot summer day hike, wear a light hat so the sun doesn't beat down on your head. Likewise, always wear sunglasses in the summer to protect your eyes. Comfortable hiking shoes are a must any time of the year. They may not be fashionable, but having aching feet is no fun no matter what the weather is.

Circle the letter of the words from the passage that signal the ways summer and winter hiking clothes are **alike**.

a. On the other hand
b. Both
c. Likewise
d. Layers

Circle the letter of the words from the passage that signal the ways summer and winter hiking clothes are **different**.

a. Protect
b. Likewise
c. Different
d. On the other hand

What things are important in **both** summer and winter hiking?

a. Gloves or mittens
b. Dress in layers
c. Comfortable shoes
d. Keep hands warm

➤ YOUR TURN

Read "Eating In and Out." While you read, look for comparisons and contrasts. Answer the questions and then complete the Venn diagram based on your answers.

Eating IN and OUT

There's no place like home when it comes to eating. Open up the refrigerator and help yourself to orange juice, milk, and eggs. A canned ham and bread are on the shelf. Need a nutritious snack for some quick energy? Fix a peanut butter and jelly sandwich. Where did all that food come from? You are probably **dependent** on stores to provide what you need. If you have planned ahead, you have the foods available that you like to eat right in your kitchen. You can help yourself to cold water or you can open the refrigerator and get some milk when you are thirsty.

What is it like to plan for food on a hike in the wilderness? When preparing for a hike, you must think ahead. Buy **nutritious** foods to keep up your energy for hiking. Another good **strategy** is to keep the food lightweight. Granola, dried fruit, and nuts are good for a quick snack. On the other hand, forget about canned hams, eggs, and milk for your hiking trip. Unlike at home, there are no refrigerators in the wilderness! Just like at home, you will get thirsty, keep in mind that the only drinkable water is what you carry with you. In both situations you can eat well, but it takes some planning.

1. Underline the words in the passage that the writer used to compare?

2. Circle the words in the passage that the writer used to contrast?

3. What comparison is the writer making in this passage.
- **a.** what the differences are between eating at home and eating in the wilderness
- **b.** how canned ham compares to granola

4. In the Venn diagram below, write in the things that are alike about eating at home and eating in the wilderness, the things that are different, and the things that they share.

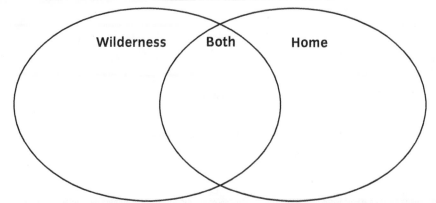

Wilderness   Both   Home

As you read, pay attention to punctuation marks that are clues to help you know when to pause.

READ on your OWN
Staying Alive, pages 42–44

Staying Alive, pages 42–44

BEFORE YOU READ

Think about the pages you just read in "How to Survive." What are some of the warning signs that a tornado is on the way?

AS YOU READ

Read pages 42–44 of "How to Survive."

Here are some statements about tornadoes. Write whether they are comparing or contrasting two things.

Statements	Comparison or contrast?	How can you tell?
Indoors or out, the goal is to make yourself as small a target as possible.		
What if a tornado warning comes while you are outdoors or in the car? Either way, abandon what you were doing.		

AFTER YOU READ

What was the most surprising thing you learned in the pages you just read? Tell why you were surprised.

VOCABULARY
Watch for the words you are learning about.

retrieve: go back and get

scant: very little or not enough

FLUENCY
Scan text for words that you many not know. Practice reading them aloud so you are comfortable pronouncing them.

TEXT STRUCTURE: Cause and Effect

How to Use Text Structure

Preview text to get an idea of its organization and purpose.

Identify the text structure. Use clues and signal words to identify problem and solution, description, sequence, cause and effect, and compare and contrast.

In some writing, you will have to **identify multiple structures** in text.

Summarize text by thinking about its structure.

Learn the STRATEGY

You have been learning about different kinds of text structures and the ways that writers organize text. You have learned that good readers look for clues that tell them how text is organized. One way that writers organize text is to use a cause-and-effect structure. A cause tells you **why** something happened. The effect is **what** happened as a result of the cause. For example, read the following sentence: *The smoke alarm started beeping because smoke was filling the room.* In this sentence the effect is that the smoke alarm started beeping. It was caused by the smoke filling the room.

Good readers know that it can be helpful to think about causes and effects to help them understand and remember how events in the text fit together. Look for words that are clues that the text may be about cause and effect. Some of these words are *because, so, since,* and *as a result.*

Read the following passage. As you read, look for examples of cause and effect. Then answer the questions.

FORCES OF NATURE

Hurricanes occur in the United States during the late summer and fall. These forces of nature result in destruction. The force of hurricane winds can knock down trees and buildings. Hurricanes' strong winds can blow at more than 100 miles per hour! People board up their windows when they know a hurricane is on the way. Many people decide to leave their homes because they want to escape the threat of a hurricane.

Which of the following phrases from the passage are **causes**?

a. forces of nature
b. destruction
c. force of wind
d. hurricane winds

Which of the following phrases from the passage are **effects**?

a. trees knocked down
b. hurricane
c. buildings knocked down
d. force of winds

YOUR TURN

Read "After a Disaster." Then answer the questions.

After a Disaster

Natural disasters, such as **torrential** hurricane rains, earthquakes, and tornadoes, can cause great damage. Because of these disasters, buildings are destroyed, trees are uprooted, and personal property is lost. However, these disasters cause more than just physical damage. They can also result in mental distress. People can feel very upset after **encountering** a traumatic event. A traumatic event is one that is very frightening. It may have effects on a person for a long time. One type of disorder is called "post-traumatic stress disorder," or PTSD.

Coping with disaster

Victims of PTSD may experience sleeplessness and stress. They may even fear being alone. What makes PTSD hard to treat is the fact that victims may not have **awareness** of their symptoms until a year after the trauma. This is what gives the disorder its name. It is post, or after, the trauma. In fact, because PTSD affects memory, it may be hard for victims to **retrieve** memories of the event that caused the disorder.

1. Which of the following can be the **cause** of physical damage and mental distress?
  a. loss of property
  b. feeling upset
  c. natural disasters

2. Which of the following are some of the **effects** of PTSD?
  a. sleeplessness
  b. loss of property
  c. stress
  d. fear of being alone

3. Now complete the cause-and-effect chart here.

CAUSE(S)	CAUSE(S)
Natural disasters	

EFFECT(S)	EFFECT(S)
	sleeplessness
	stress
	fear of being alone

To keep your reading lively, change your tone of voice to match the content of what you are reading.

FLUENCY

READ on your OWN
Staying Alive, pages 45–48

BEFORE YOU READ

Think about what you just read in "How to Survive." Why is it important to go to a sheltered place in case of a tornado?

AS YOU READ

Read pages 45–48.
Use the information in the pages you just read to complete the cause-and-effect chart below.

CAUSE(S)	CAUSE(S)	CAUSE(S)
There are hurricane rains and giant waves.	Wind gusts reach 74 mph.	

EFFECT(S)	EFFECT(S)	EFFECT(S)
		People usually have time to get away.

AFTER YOU READ

What was the most surprising information you read in this section?

Make Words Yours!

Learn the WORDS

As you read more about ways to survive natural disasters, you'll come across these words. This is your chance to get to know them better.

WORD AND EXPLANATION	EXAMPLE	WRITE AN EXAMPLE
When you **abandon** something, you give it up or leave it.	In a fire, it is better to **abandon** your home than to risk your life.	When might you need to **abandon** a plan?
Something is **available** when it is ready for use or easy to get.	Hamburgers are only **available** in our cafeteria on Tuesdays.	What resources might not be **available** during a disaster?
Something **established** is set up or firmly put into place. Governments are **established**. So are laws.	Emergency centers are often **established** in gyms or other locations.	What procedures has your school **established** for emergencies?
A **majority** is more than half of the people or things in a group.	In a school of 100 students, 51 or more students is a **majority**.	How do you spend the **majority** of your time?
To **recommend** is to strongly suggest or advise.	The authorities **recommend** that you get out of the path of a hurricane.	What after-school activities would you **recommend** to friends?
When you **reserve** something, you set it aside for later use.	Hikers usually **reserve** some food for the walk home.	How could you **reserve** water for an emergency?
If you **retain** something, you keep it. You **retain** memories. You might **retain** old toys.	In a snowstorm, it can be hard to **retain** your sense of direction.	How can you **retain** information that you just read?
Temporary means for a short time. Something **temporary** changes or goes away.	Luckily, Jamir's knee injury was only a **temporary** setback.	If you could have a **temporary** job, what would it be?

YOUR TURN

Answer these questions and be ready to explain your answers.

1. If three out of six people vote for something, is it a *majority*? _____

2. Should life vests be *available* on all boats? _____

3. Can a wall be built to *retain* water? _____

4. Did you ever *recommend* something that turned out to be a bad idea? _____

Choose the right word

abandon	available	established	majority
recommend	reserve	temporary	retain

Fill each blank with the correct word from the box.

5. I could never _____ my pets in a crisis.

6. The _____ of people in the area have not experienced a tornado.

7. Use every _____ tool to make your home safe.

8. An oven can _____ heat.

9. People moved into _____ shelters during the flood.

10. Emergency services _____ a command post to coordinate rescue efforts.

11. The authorities _____ that you _____ a supply of bottled water.

Show that you know what to do during an emergency by completing the sentences.

Show that you know

Complete the sentences.

12. Supplies that you should *reserve* in case of a hurricane include

13. A stay in a *temporary* shelter can

14. In an emergency, you may have to *abandon*

15. Shelters are often *established* in

READ on your OWN
Staying Alive, pages 49–51

BEFORE YOU READ

Think about the pages you just read in "How to Survive." Why is it helpful to be able to predict a hurricane?

AS YOU READ

Read pages 49–51 of "How to Survive."
Use the information in the pages you just read to complete the cause-and-effect chart below.

CAUSE(S)	CAUSE(S)	CAUSE(S)
Hurricane rains stir up wind and water.	Flooding and dangerous currents appeared.	

EFFECT(S)	EFFECT(S)	EFFECT(S)
		It swept away half of the island's homes.

AFTER YOU READ

Why do you think it is important to pay attention when officials issue warnings about disasters on the way?

VOCABULARY
Watch for the words you are learning about.

recommend: suggest something is good

retain: to hold on to

abandoned: left alone

established: begun, set up

FLUENCY
Watch punctuation. Pause briefly for commas, and longer for periods.

TEXT STRUCTURE: Using Clues to Identify Structures

How to Use Text Structure

Preview text to get an idea of its organization and purpose.

Identify the text structure. Use clues and signal words to identify problem and solution, description, sequence, cause and effect and compare and contrast.

In some writing, you will have to **identify multiple structures** in text.

Summarize text by thinking about its structure.

Learn the STRATEGY

Good readers know that recognizing which type of structure an author has used helps them understand and recall what they read. Writers may use several different structures in the same text. For example, one paragraph may have a cause-and-effect structure. Another may be structured according to problem and solution. If you can identify the structure, it will help you remember what you read.

Sometimes a heading or words in the text are clues about the text structure. For example, say you preview the text. You see words such as *first, then, next, before,* and *late.* That suggests the details are in a sequence. Words such as *because* or *as a result* may mean that the author is using a cause-and-effect text structure.

Read the passage below. Look for clues that help you identify text structure.

STEPS IN SURVIVAL TRAINING

Modern soldiers have to go through survival training. What kinds of things do the soldiers learn? First, they have to learn how to find food, shelter, and tools in areas where none are readily available. Next, soldiers are taught to keep their minds clear. Soldiers in survival situations have to concentrate on what they are doing. Finally, they have to learn how to alert rescuers so they can be found. Even though they have great survival skills and can keep themselves alive, soldiers may need to be rescued and brought to safety.

Which of the following text structures did you identify in the passage?

a. sequence
b. compare and contrast
c. fact and opinion

Which of the following clues did you use to decide on the structure you identified?

a. the writer's opinion
b. signal words in the heading
c. signal words in the text

YOUR TURN

Read "A Pilot's Fight to Survive." As you read, think about how the writer structured the text. Then answer the questions.

A Pilot's Fight to SURVIVE

Shot Down Captain Scott O'Grady is an American fighter pilot. He was shot down over Bosnia during a peacekeeping mission. O'Grady's F-16 jet was hit by surface-to-air missiles on June 2, 1995. As a result, he landed in a forest, where he hid for days. He knew he would be either captured or rescued.

Trained to Survive As part of his military training, O'Grady had learned survival techniques. During the survival training O'Grady had been left cold and hungry in the mountains of northeast Washington state. He learned to eat black ants and grasshoppers. He learned how to make tools from branches and to create a shelter. He also carried a special chart **reserved** for emergencies. It listed edible plants and how to cook them. He used the chart and his training to survive for 6 days. He also learned how to use a radio signal.

A Daring Rescue On June 8, O'Grady was able to use his radio to signal for help. Upon receiving Captain O'Grady's distress call, his rescuers risked a rescue in daylight. They knew that flying during the day was dangerous and not **recommended**. However, O'Grady was in danger of capture at any time. Therefore, they decided it was the only solution. If they did not attempt a daytime rescue, O'Grady was at risk of being captured. They took the risk and as a result, they saved his life. The story of Captain O'Grady is a tribute to his training. His rescuers were not willing to **abandon** him, and he **retained** the will to survive until he could be rescued.

1. Reread the first paragraph. How does the writer organize it?
   a. compare and contrast
   b. cause and effect
   c. problem and solution

What clues helped you decide?

2. Now reread the second paragraph. What kind of text structure does the writer use?

What clues helped you decide?

3. Reread the third paragraph. What kind of text structure does the writer use?

What clues helped you decide?

When reading aloud, try to use the same tone and pace that you would use in conversation. FLUENCY

READ on your OWN
Staying Alive, pages 52–55

BEFORE YOU READ

Think about the pages you just read in "How to Survive." What kinds of problems can arise *after* a hurricane has passed by?

AS YOU READ

Read pages 52–55 of "How to Survive."
In the chart below, for each statement write whether it is a cause or an effect.

VOCABULARY
Watch for the words you are learning about.

reserve: set aside for future use

available: ready for use or easy to obtain

retain: to hold in place

abandon: to give up

FLUENCY
Keep your voice natural while you read, as if you were speaking to a friend.

Statements	Cause or effect?
They were trapped by unusually heavy snowstorms they encountered.	
Almost half the group died of hunger and cold.	
Like hurricanes, winter storms can usually be predicted.	
That makes it possible to take precautions.	
The layers trap air that will help retain warmth.	
Wear several layers of clothes.	

AFTER YOU READ

What was something new you learned in the section that you just read?

Get Wordwise!
Connotation

Learn More About the WORDS

A word's dictionary definition is called its **denotation**. Many words also have **connotations**. A word's connotation is the emotional image the word creates. Words with almost the same definition can have very different connotations.

Climbing that hill was **challenging**!

Climbing that hill was **difficult**!

Challenging and *difficult* have almost the same dictionary meaning. They are synonyms that describe something that takes hard work or skill to do. However, there is a big difference in their connotations. *Challenging* describes something that you want to do because you are excited about it. *Difficult* describes something that may cause a problem because it is hard to do.

WORD	WORD IN A SENTENCE	WHAT'S THE CONNOTATION?	
scant	Food supplies were **scant**, and the animals looked thin.	☐ positive	☐ negative
error	No matter how hard you try, it's almost impossible to do every job without making an **error**.	☐ positive	☐ negative
prosper	People can **prosper** even if they don't have a lot of money.	☐ positive	☐ negative
abandon	The builders **abandoned** the project when they were only half finished.	☐ positive	☐ negative
clarity	After being confused for weeks about what to do, Ana suddenly got **clarity** from the new directions.	☐ positive	☐ negative

YOUR TURN

What's the connotation?

Below are some words you have studied before. Decide whether they have positive or negative connotations.

1. mutual _____

2. plunder _____

3. recommend _____

4. recover _____

5. sincere _____

6. destructive _____

7. heritage _____

8. nutritious _____

Right or Wrong?

Read the sentences below. Decide whether each underlined word is used the right way or the wrong way.

9. The fog came in very quickly, and drivers were surprised by the <u>clarity</u>. _____

10. If supplies are <u>scant</u>, there will be enough for everyone. _____

11. To <u>guarantee</u> shows that you believe something will happen. _____

12. Kim's summer project <u>prospered</u>, and the kids who took part learned a lot. _____

13. I can't get enough of my puppy, and the feeling seems to be <u>mutual</u>. _____

14. The shop had clearly been <u>plundered</u>, and we spent an hour looking at the beautiful displays. _____

15. Tiara <u>recommends</u> that we all try out for the play. _____

16. The snacks were <u>nutritious</u>, but we ate them anyway. _____

17. The country's <u>heritage</u> went back over a thousand years. _____

You've read about how to prepare for natural disasters. What advice would you give to someone about preparing for the worst?

Show that you know

Use each word in a sentence.

18. recommend

19. abandon

20. recover

21. destructive

READ on your OWN
Staying Alive, pages 56–58

VOCABULARY
Watch for the words you are learning about.

majority: most of

abandoning: leaving

temporary: for a while, not always

FLUENCY
Preview text before you read aloud. That way, if there are words you don't know you can practice saying them.

BEFORE YOU READ

Think about the pages you just read in "How to Survive." What are some things to keep in a car if you drive during a storm?

AS YOU READ

Read pages 56–58 of "How to Survive."
In the chart below, for each section of text, write whether the structure is problem/solution or cause and effect. Put an X in the correct column.

Text	Problem/solution	Cause and effect
Power outages can occur in any season due to storms or temporary problems at utility companies.		
Blackouts can also result from earthquakes, tornadoes, and hurricanes.		
Another priority is to prevent food from spoiling. Move perishable items from the refrigerator to the freezer or an ice chest.		

AFTER YOU READ

Do you think you would be able to remain calm in the face of disaster? Explain why or why not.

TEXT STRUCTURE: Summarize

How to Use Text Structure

Preview text to get an idea of its organization and purpose.

Identify the text structure. Use clues and signal words to identify problem and solution, description, sequence, cause and effect, and compare and contrast.

In some writing, you will have to **identify multiple structures** in text.

Summarize text by thinking about its structure.

Learn the STRATEGY

You have been learning about different kinds of text structure in this unit. You have seen how some writers organize what they write. When good readers recognize the structure of the text they read, it helps them summarize what they have read.

Summarizing means retelling something in few words. When you summarize, you remember and understand what you have read. A good way to think about a summary is to first ask yourself about the structure of the text you have read. Did the writer use compare and contrast, cause and effect, or another structure? Look for clues in the text to help you identify the structure.

Read the passage below. Try to identify the text structure the writer uses.

GOOD SENSE IN EXTREME WEATHER

Both heat waves and very cold weather can harm people. Some people need special care during extremes of both hot and cold weather. These people include very young children or elderly persons who are already sick. It is important that when the weather is very cold, these people's homes have enough heat. Those without heat in extremely cold weather may suffer from frostbite, which is damage to fingers and toes. On the other hand, during a heat wave, these people need a cool, airy place to go. They must avoid getting overheated. Having a fan or air conditioner can be important.

What text structures did the author use in the passage?

a. sequence
b. Compare and contrast

What things are being compared and contrasted in the passage?

a. elderly people and very small children
b. water pipes and electricity supplies
c. heat waves and extreme cold

Which words signal that heat waves and cold weather are being contrasted?

a. both
b. on the other hand
c. strain

Which is the best summary of the passage?

a. This passage compares elderly people and young children.
b. This passage compares and contrasts what can happen in extreme heat and cold.
c. This passage contrasts cold weather and hot weather.

YOUR TURN

Read "Illnesses From Heat," and answer the questions. Be sure to pay attention to signal words that are clues about the text structures that the writer uses.

1. What text structure is suggested in this paragraph?
  a. compare/contrast
  b. sequence
  c. fact and opinion

How can you tell?

2. What text structure is suggested in this paragraph?
  a. problem/solution
  b. sequence
  c. cause and effect

How can you tell?

Illnesses From Heat

To keep safe during a heat wave, it is important to be aware of the signs of heat illness. Two main types of illness caused by extreme heat are heat exhaustion and heat stroke. They have similarities and differences.

Heat Stroke During heat stroke the body's temperature-control system stops working. If the victim is not cooled immediately, brain damage and even death may result. What are signs of heatstroke? They include very high body temperature, red skin, changes in consciousness, weak pulse, and rapid shallow breathing. Once it is **established** a person has heat stroke, get him or her to a cool place, and call 911 immediately.

Heat Exhaustion Heat exhaustion is less severe. It is usually **temporary**, but it can lead to heat stroke. Symptoms include heavy sweating, nausea and vomiting, headache, and dizziness. The victim may also feel extremely tired. Body temperature may be normal, but it will rise.

To treat heat exhaustion, first move the victim to an **available** cool place. Then loosen or remove tight clothing. Finally, give the person liquids every 15 minutes. The majority of heat exhaustion victims recover quickly but feel very tired afterward.

3. How would you summarize what this passage is about if you were explaining it to a friend?

As you read and reread, pay attention to punctuation marks.

FLUENCY

READ on your OWN
Staying Alive, pages 59–61

BEFORE YOU READ

Think about the pages you read in "How to Survive." What are some of the difficult things that happen *after* a disaster is over?

AS YOU READ

Read pages 59–61 in "How to Survive."
Read each set of statements. Then circle the kind of text structure it shows.

Statements	Text structure
In the worst cases, families may not be able to return home at all. They will establish bases somewhere else.	Problem and solution Fact and opinion Compare and contrast
It's normal to feel upset when scary things happen.	Problem and solution Cause and effect Compare and contrast

VOCABULARY
Watch for the words you are learning about.

established: set up

temporary: just for a while, not permanent

retention: being saved or kept

available: able to have or get

FLUENCY
Pause briefly when you come to a comma and longer at a period.

AFTER YOU READ

What was the most interesting thing you learned in the pages you just read? Why did you think it was interesting?

Unit 4 Reflection

VOCABULARY

The easiest part of learning new words is

The hardest part is

I still need to work on

Staying Alive

COMPREHENSION

The step that helped me the most with text structure is

The hardest thing about text structure is

I still need to work on

FLUENCY

I read most fluently when

I still need to work on

INDEPENDENT READING

My favorite part of Staying Alive is

Strange Journeys

COMPREHENSION
LEARN A VARIETY OF VISUALIZING TECHNIQUES

unit 5

INDEPENDENT READING
Strange Journeys
Includes "Colliding With the Future"
and "Weird Places"

VOCABULARY

WORDS:
Know them!
Use them!
Learn all about them!

FLUENCY
Make your reading
smooth and accurate,
one tip at a time

Make Words Yours!

Learn the WORDS

Here are some words you will be reading in the next week. They are also words you will need to know for your everyday reading.

WORD AND EXPLANATION	EXAMPLE	WRITE AN EXAMPLE
When you **arrange** things, you put them in a certain order.	Ebony **arranged** the plate of cookies so that the nicest ones were on top.	How do you **arrange** your activities on the weekends?
To **conclude** is to form an opinion or make a decision about something after careful thinking.	Because I am hungry, I **conclude** that it's time to eat.	What can you **conclude** about the importance of being on time?
Acting **conspicuously** is acting in a way that brings attention.	Samantha walked **conspicuously** into the room and turned to show off her new outfit.	When might you want to do something **conspicuously**?
A **destination** is where someone or something is going.	The traveler's **destination** was Mexico.	What **destination** would you choose for a dream vacation?
When you **reason**, you think through something in a logical way.	Jake and Zack **reasoned** that they should split the money because they each did half the work.	When is the last time you **reasoned** with a friend?
Scanning is looking over something quickly.	Maya is **scanning** the book to see which part she needs to read first.	If you are **scanning** an advertisement, what might you be looking for?
When you **theorize**, you make a guess based on facts.	Scientists **theorize** about what happened to the dinosaurs.	What do you like to **theorize** about?
To **transport** something is to move it from one place to another.	The space shuttle **transports** astronauts to the space station.	What do you use to **transport** your stuff to school?

YOUR TURN

Answer these questions and be ready to explain your answers.

1. Could your *destination* be the place you just came from? _____

2. Could you *theorize* about something if you don't have any facts? _____

3. If your best friend didn't talk to you, would you *conclude* that he or she was mad at you? _____

4. If you are *scanning* a page, are you reading every word? _____

Choose the right word

> arrange   conclude   conspicuously   reason
> theorize   scanning   destination   transport

Fill each blank with the correct word from the box.

5. It took four vans to _____ all of us to the game.

6. Maria was able to _____ her way out of being grounded.

7. I couldn't help but _____ that she was lost because she was alone.

8. I thought I could help by _____ the parking lot for the girl's mother.

9. Everyone noticed that Wanda was waving her arms _____ .

10. Our gym teacher asked us to _____ ourselves by size.

11. I could only _____ about why Ben did what he did.

12. Our _____ was Josh's party.

Show that you know the words by completing sentences about what it might be like to travel into the future.

Show that you know

Complete the sentences.

13. Someone might be *conspicuously* out of place if he or she traveled into the future because

14. It could be *reasoned* that life in the future

15. If people wanted to travel into the future, they would need to *arrange* for

16. If I were *transported* into the future, I would

READ on your OWN
Strange Journeys, pages 3–7

BEFORE YOU READ

Look at the selection title and think about the future. What picture do you see in your mind when you read the title?

AS YOU READ

Read "Who Is Finton Fenton?" pages 3–7. (STOP)
Draw a picture of what you think Finton Fenton looks like. Make sure you use details from the story.

VOCABULARY
Watch for the words you are learning about.

conspicuously: in a way that draws attention

theories: guesses that are based on facts

conclude: to decide

conspicuous: impossible to overlook

conclusion: a decision

concluded: decided

FLUENCY
In order to read smoothly, practice pronouncing each character's name before you start to read.

AFTER YOU READ

What would you have done at the old house?

VISUALIZE: Use Pictures to Understand

How to Visualize

Use pictures to help you visualize what the passage does and does not tell you.

Find descriptive and sensory words and use them to form pictures in your mind of what you are reading.

Draw conclusions after forming pictures in your mind about what you are reading.

Visualize a sequence of events to help you understand what you are reading.

Use visual aids, such as graphic organizers, to help you understand what you are reading.

Learn the STRATEGY

Have you ever heard the saying "A picture is worth a thousand words"? You can gather a lot of information by looking at a picture. For example, a photograph of a family may show the number of people in the family, their ages, and what they enjoy doing together.

When reading a book, use the pictures to help you understand what you are reading. Examine each picture carefully. Then ask yourself, "What does the picture tell me about the meaning of this part of the book?"

Read the passage below and look at the picture. Think about how the picture helps you understand the words.

Randy's neighbor, Mr. Henson, had been working on his car for weeks. When he was working, the garage door was always closed. Then one day, Randy happened to walk by when the garage door was up for just a minute. He got a quick look at the weirdest-looking car he'd ever seen. It had six tailpipes and several V-shaped antennas. Either Mr. Henson wasn't much of a mechanic or something strange was going on.

How did the picture help you understand what you read?

_____

_____

_____

_____

_____

➤ YOUR TURN

Read "Driving Into the Future."
Use the picture to help you
understand the story.

---

1. How does the picture on this page help you to understand the story?

---

2. On a separate sheet of paper, draw a picture to show how Randy's house may have changed from the beginning to the end of the boys' ride in Mr. Henson's car. Then use your picture to explain the story to another student.

DRIVING ▶▶
INTO THE FUTURE

One afternoon, Randy and his friend Alex were shooting hoops in Randy's driveway. Suddenly, Mr. Henson opened his garage door and backed his car out. Randy could see that Mr. Henson had **arranged** the antennas in a row on the roof of the car. Randy and Alex wanted to get a better look at the car. They didn't want to be too **conspicuous** about it, though. Randy purposely threw the ball over Alex's head so that it landed near the car. They both ran over to get the ball.

Mr. Henson rolled down the car window and leaned his head out. He said, "Would you boys like to take a quick spin around the neighborhood?"

The boys **reasoned** that they had time for a short ride before dinner, so they hopped into the backseat. They were amazed by the huge number of gadgets and gauges on the dashboard. Mr. Henson drove very slowly around the block a few times. Randy and Alex were starting to get bored. Then they noticed that the houses on their block suddenly looked different. Randy's blue house was now red. Alex's green house was bright yellow. Then the houses started to go by in a blur, even though it didn't feel as if the car was going faster.

After several minutes, Mr. Henson stopped the car and looked back at the boys. They sat wide-eyed with wonder. He pointed to a gauge that read 2050. He explained that the gauge showed the year. The car had **transported** them to the future, but they were still in their neighborhood. That explained why the houses looked so different!

Pay attention to punctuation. Pause before and after a phrase that is separated by commas from the rest of the sentence.

FLUENCY

READ on your OWN
Strange Journeys, pages 8–10

BEFORE YOU READ

Think about what you read in Chapter 1 of "Colliding With the Future." Why did the four friends go inside Finton Fenton's house?

AS YOU READ

Read "The Mystery Grows," pages 8–10.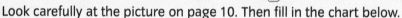
Look carefully at the picture on page 10. Then fill in the chart below.

VOCABULARY

Watch for the words you are learning about.

reasoned: decided in a logical way

inconspicuous: not easily noticeable

theorize: to make a guess based on facts

destination: a place where a person is going or where an object is being sent

theory: a guess that is based on facts

FLUENCY

Pay attention to punctuation. Use commas to help you read long sentences.

What the picture shows	How the picture helped me understand the chapter

AFTER YOU READ

Choose the character in the story you think is most like you and explain why.

Get Wordwise!
More Word Families

Learn More About the WORDS

Below are some words you have studied, along with other words from the same **word families**. As you know, all the words in a word family have the same base word. Knowing the meaning of one word in a word family will help you understand the meaning of the other words in that word family.

ARRANGE

To **arrange** is to put things in order according to a plan.

When you are **arranging** things, you are putting them
☐ in boxes to get them out of the way.
☐ in a certain order.

An **arrangement** of flowers is
☐ carefully thought out.
☐ scattered on the ground.

CONCLUDE

To **conclude** is to form an opinion after careful thinking. To **conclude** also means to end.

When you are **concluding** a speech, you are
☐ finishing it.
☐ starting it.

The **conclusion** of a report is intended to
☐ introduce it.
☐ bring it to a close.

DESTINATION

Your **destination** is the place where you plan to go. It is the end of a trip.

Your **destiny** is something that you are meant
☐ to watch.
☐ to do.

If you feel you are **destined** to do something, you feel
☐ that you can't do it.
☐ that it will happen in the end.

REASON

To **reason** is to decide about something in a logical way.

A **reasonable** person
☐ thinks things through.
☐ acts without thinking.

Someone who is acting **reasonably** is
☐ acting silly.
☐ acting with a plan.

THEORIZE

To **theorize** is to make a guess that is based on facts.

A **theory** is
☐ a fact about something.
☐ an idea based on information.

A concept is **theoretical** if it is
☐ not proven beyond a doubt.
☐ proven beyond a doubt.

TRANSPORT

To **transport** is to move something or someone from one place to another.

One mode of **transportation** is
☐ a car.
☐ a telephone.

A **transporter** moves things
☐ around on a table.
☐ from place to place.

►YOUR TURN

Choose the right word

> conclusion   transportation   destined
> arranging   arrangement   reasonable

Fill each blank with the correct word from the box.

1. Gabriele made an [_____] of seashells.

2. I thought that my request was completely [_____].

3. Sam seems [_____] to become a teacher because he loves to explain things.

4. We used public [_____] to get downtown.

5. The [_____] of the game against the Tigers was exciting.

6. In math class, we are [_____] triangles to form different shapes.

Which word works?

Circle the correct word in each pair.

7. Alia uses a stroller to **transportation** / **transport** her little brother.

8. Jon was **arranging** / **arrangement** the papers in alphabetical order.

9. We have **conclusion** / **concluded** that the answer can't be found.

10. I believe it is the **destination** / **destiny** of the soccer team to win the championship.

11. Josef was acting **reasonable** / **reasonably** when he offered us a ride home.

12. I have a **theory** / **theoretical** about what the results of my science project will be.

> Have you ever imagined that you could travel through time? Show that you know the words as you imagine time travel.

Show that you know

Complete the sentences.

13. If I were traveling through time, I would like my *transporter* to take me

14. An *arrangement* I would need to make before traveling through time is

15. Before *concluding* my time travel, I would like to

16. Even though time travel is only *theoretical*, I wish

READ on your OWN
Strange Journeys, pages 11–13

BEFORE YOU READ

Think about what you read in Chapter 2. Where did the four friends wind up at the end of the chapter?

AS YOU READ

Read "What on Earth?" pages 11–13.
Look carefully at the picture on page 12. Then fill in the chart below.

What the picture shows	How the picture helped me understand the chapter

VOCABULARY
Watch for the words you are learning about.

transported: carried from one place to another

reasoned: decided in a logical way

destination: the place where a person is going or where an object is being sent

FLUENCY
Be careful to read every word so that the text will make sense.

AFTER YOU READ

How would you react if you traveled to the future and got stuck there?

VISUALIZE: Use Descriptive Words

How to Visualize

Use pictures to help you visualize what the passage does and does not tell you.

Find descriptive and sensory words and use them to form pictures in your mind of what you are reading.

Draw conclusions after forming pictures in your mind about what you are reading.

Visualize a sequence of events to help you understand what you are reading.

Use visual aids, such as graphic organizers, to help you understand what you are reading.

Learn the STRATEGY

You have seen that pictures can help you understand what you are reading. Not all books or passages include pictures, though. Good readers try to create their own pictures by visualizing what they are reading. Visualizing means creating pictures in one's mind. You can use descriptive words to help you visualize what is described. For example, consider the phrase "the dry and shriveled apple." You can use the words *dry* and *shriveled* to "see" an apple that is old and wrinkled.

Read each paragraph below and underline the descriptive words. Use the underlined words to form a picture in your mind of the scene.

Paragraph 1

Jamal looked excitedly at the new sneakers on his feet. With the push of a button, the soles of the black sneakers would expand and add 4 inches to his height! With eager fingers, Jamal pushed the button on the heel. The sneakers pushed him slowly upward. He ran to a mirror and breathed a relieved sigh. He looked terrific!

Paragraph 2

Jamal looked anxiously at the new sneakers on his feet. With the push of a button, the soles of the orange sneakers would expand and add 12 inches to his height! With trembling fingers, Jamal pushed the button on the heel. The sneakers pushed him rapidly upward. He ran to a mirror and breathed a disappointed sigh. He looked ridiculous!

How did your mental picture change from Paragraph 1 to Paragraph 2?

_____

_____

_____

_____

_____

_____

Compare the descriptive words in the two paragraphs. How do the different words change the meaning of the paragraphs?

_____

_____

_____

_____

_____

_____

_____

_____

The Old Journal

Read "The Old Journal."
Use the descriptive words
to help you understand
the story.

1. Underline the descriptive words and phrases in the passage. Use the words and phrases to create pictures in your mind of the passage.

2. On a separate sheet of paper, draw a picture of one of the pictures you formed in your mind as you read the passage. Then list the descriptive words and phrases that helped you create the image.

Tana lifted the musty leather journal from the drawer. The date 2025 was printed in gold on the leather cover. She carefully turned the brittle, yellow pages. Then she studied the bold, blue handwriting. Tana was very excited to see and touch paper because it had been banned centuries ago. The vast woodlands that had once been harvested to make paper had been turned into farms. Farms, and not forests, were the top priority in the overpopulated world of 2525. Tana opened the journal and began to eagerly **scan** its contents.

*This afternoon, I had to trudge through deep snow to the shopping mall. I would have liked to stay in front of the roaring fire. I planned on sipping a cup of steaming hot chocolate and listening to my favorite CDs. Today is Mom's birthday, though. I had put off getting her gift until the last minute. Then we had an unexpected snowstorm! I was half-frozen by the time I reached my **destination**. I think I found the perfect gift, though—a silky, lavender scarf with a purple fringe. It was expensive, at least for a teenager like myself. I **concluded**, however, that Mom would love it.*

Tana laughed softly to herself. Today was her mom's birthday, and she still needed to buy a gift! "It's 2525, but I guess teenage girls aren't that much different now than they were in 2025," she **theorized**. "We are still waiting until the very last minute to get things done!"

Be careful to read every word without skipping or substituting words.

FLUENCY

READ on your OWN
Strange Journeys, pages 14–16

BEFORE YOU READ

Think about what you read in Chapter 3. Why can't the four friends go back in time?

AS YOU READ

Read "Lots of Bots," pages 14–16.
Then list the descriptive phrases in the last paragraph on page 14. Draw a picture of a mental image you formed as you read the paragraph.

VOCABULARY
Watch for the words you are learning about.

transported: carried from one place to another

scanning: looking at something quickly

reasoned: decided in a logical way

arrange: to put in proper order

scanned: looked at quickly

FLUENCY
To read smoothly, read every word and do not skip or substitute words.

Descriptive phrases in the last paragraph	My mental image

AFTER YOU READ

Choose the most interesting event in this chapter and explain your choice.

Make Words Yours!

Learn the WORDS

Here are some words you will be reading in the next week. They are also words you will meet in your everyday reading.

WORD AND EXPLANATION	EXAMPLE	WRITE AN EXAMPLE
A **consolation** is something that comforts you and makes you feel better.	My brother's hug was a nice **consolation** after I dropped out of the spelling bee.	What could be a **consolation** after a ball game is rained out?
A **consultation** is a meeting in which someone is seeking information or advice.	My **consultation** with the school counselor helped me think about my future.	What might you want to find out in a **consultation** with a personal trainer?
A **filter** is a device that removes or separates dirt or other unwanted things from liquids or gases.	A water **filter** strains out harmful things that you can't see.	What kinds of **filters** can you buy in stores?
To **hover** is to float or hang in the air over something.	A hummingbird **hovered** over the flower.	What else can **hover**?
To **input** is to contribute or put in something, such as data or ideas. **Input** is a contribution.	Erik's parents asked for his **input** on where to go for vacation.	Why is it good to give **input** into a group project?
When you **pinpoint** something, you find its exact place and time.	I was able to **pinpoint** the location where I lost my wallet.	How could the exact time you were born be **pinpointed**?
When you make a **revision** to something, you change it, usually for the better.	Teri made **revisions** to her essay before handing it in.	What is something you have done a **revision** of?
Suitably means in a proper or right way.	Dad was **suitably** impressed by the music program.	What would you wear to be **suitably** dressed for gym?

YOUR TURN

Yes or No?

Answer these questions and be ready to explain your answers.

1. Can you have a *consultation* with someone your own age? _____

2. Would you be *suitably* dressed if you wore jeans to a wedding? _____

3. Can you *pinpoint* the last time you sneezed? _____

4. Do you *filter* out sunlight if you wear dark glasses? _____

5. Would a *revision* of a book have the same subject as the original? _____

6. Would a person who isn't sad or upset need *consolation*? _____

7. If your friend had a problem, would you give your *input*? _____

8. Can an airplane *hover* in one place? _____

Choose the right word

consolation   consultation   filter
pinpoint   revision   suitably

Answer each riddle with the best word.

9. Which word is a change in something to make it better? [_____]

10. Which word might make you feel better? [_____]

11. Which word gets rid of unwanted stuff? [_____]

12. Which word lets you know exactly when or where? [_____]

13. Which word tells if it's being done properly? [_____]

14. Which word is a meeting where someone learns something or gets some advice? [_____]

Show that you know the words by making some guesses about the future.

Show that you know

Complete the sentences.

15. People might *hover* over the ground in _____

16. People might *input* data into _____

READ on your OWN
Strange Journeys, pages 17–19

BEFORE YOU READ

Think about what you read in Chapter 4. What has happened to the planet Earth by 2525?

AS YOU READ

Read "Reported," pages 17–19.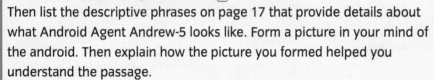
Then list the descriptive phrases on page 17 that provide details about what Android Agent Andrew-5 looks like. Form a picture in your mind of the android. Then explain how the picture you formed helped you understand the passage.

VOCABULARY
Watch for the words you are learning about.

filtering: passing something through a device that separates out unwanted material

hovered: hung in the air

consulted: sought information or advice from someone

filter: to pass something through a device that separates out unwanted material

FLUENCY
Watch for quotation marks. Read the quoted words as the speaker would say them.

Descriptive phrases	How my picture helped me understand

AFTER YOU READ

How would you react if you found out that an asteroid was on a direct path to hit Earth?

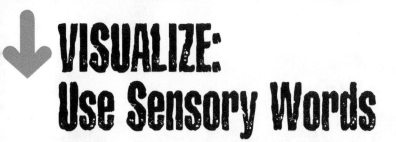

VISUALIZE: Use Sensory Words

How to Visualize

Use pictures to help you visualize what the passage does and does not tell you.

Find descriptive and sensory words and use them to form pictures in your mind of what you are reading.

Draw conclusions after forming pictures in your mind about what you are reading.

Visualize a sequence of events to help you understand what you are reading.

Use visual aids, such as graphic organizers, to help you understand what you are reading.

Learn the STRATEGY

Sensory words are words that connect to our five senses. They help us to create a sense that we can see, hear, taste, smell, and feel what is described. You can use sensory words to create pictures in your mind and thoughts about what you read. Consider, for example, this sentence.

The sudden rain shower drummed softly on Sasha's bare head.

Now use the sensory phrase *drummed softly* to "see" and "hear" the raindrops as they fall.

Read the passage below and underline the sensory words and phrases.

I woke up to the buzz of my alarm clock. I jumped right out of bed. Zerbo, my new robot, was being delivered this morning. I wanted to be ready for him! I had barely finished breakfast when the doorbell started ringing. When I opened the door, I saw the delivery robot. It was dragging a rough, lopsided crate.

It took several minutes to pry open the wooden crate, but finally my robot was free. He was wonderful! His shiny, metal exterior glowed, and he smelled like oil and fresh paint. He had a dozen flashing buttons on a square panel in the center of his chest. When I pushed the bright red "start" button, I heard a faint whirring sound. His eyes popped open and he said in a gravelly voice, "You must be Calvin, my new human."

Use the sensory words you underlined to form a picture in your mind of the scene.

Describe the picture you formed in your mind.

_____

_____

_____

_____

_____

_____

How does the picture in your mind help you to understand the scene described in the text?

_____

_____

_____

_____

YOUR TURN

Read "Not a Perfect Match!" Use the sensory words to help you understand the story.

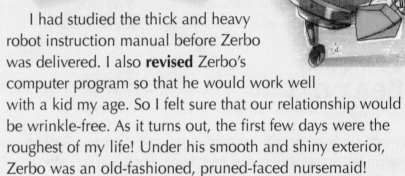

Not a Perfect Match!

1. Reread the passage. Then underline the sensory words and phrases. Use some of the sensory words and phrases to form a picture in your mind of the scene. List the sensory words you used.

2. Describe the picture you formed in your mind. Then tell how you used some of the sensory words in the passage to form your picture.

I had studied the thick and heavy robot instruction manual before Zerbo was delivered. I also **revised** Zerbo's computer program so that he would work well with a kid my age. So I felt sure that our relationship would be wrinkle-free. As it turns out, the first few days were the roughest of my life! Under his smooth and shiny exterior, Zerbo was an old-fashioned, pruned-faced nursemaid!

The trouble started on the day he was delivered. It was a warm and sunny Saturday in spring. The sweet-smelling lilac blossoms glowed in the **filtered** light of early morning. I just had to be outside for a few minutes, so I figured I'd shoot a few hoops before starting my weekend homework. Zerbo followed me outside and **hovered** nearby. After just a few minutes, Zerbo's lights starting flashing. He began to repeat "Off schedule. Time for homework" in a droning voice. I tried to drown him out by singing loudly, but it was no use. He just got loud, too. Finally, I gave up, went to my room, and started my homework. Of course, Zerbo followed me. He started **pinpointing** every tiny mess in my room. His lights began blinking like crazy as he scooped up my dirty laundry from the floor. All the while, he kept repeating "Unacceptable, disorderly room" in a scolding voice. I groaned out loud. Was this the same robot I had been looking forward to so eagerly?

Notice changes in the author's tone and match it with the expression in your voice.

FLUENCY

READ on your OWN
Strange Journeys, pages 20–22

VOCABULARY
Watch for the words you are learning about.

pinpointed: found exactly

suitable: fitting or proper

pinpoint: to find exactly

input: to put in

revisions: changes

FLUENCY
When you read dialogue, match the character's tone or mood.

BEFORE YOU READ

Think about what you read in Chapter 5. What do the four friends learn at the end of the chapter?

AS YOU READ

Read "Collision Course," pages 20–22.
Find the sensory phrases in the first paragraph on page 21.
List the phrases in the chart below. Use them to create a mental image.
Then draw a picture of the image you formed.

Sensory words in the first paragraph	My mental image

AFTER YOU READ

Choose the part of this chapter that you found most interesting and explain why.

Get Wordwise!
The Prefixes *re-*, *dis-*, *pre-*, and *con-*

Learn More About the WORDS

You have learned that a **prefix** is a word part added to the beginning of a word and that a prefix changes a word's meaning.

re- means again	To <u>re</u>construct is to build something *again*.
dis- means not or opposite	To <u>dis</u>cover is to find or uncover— the *opposite* of cover.
pre- means before	A <u>pre</u>fix comes before a word.

Look at how prefixes change the meanings of some words you have studied.

WORD AND MEANING	ADD THE PREFIX
continue: to keep on doing something	If you stop doing something, you _____**continue** it.
possess: to have or own something	To take back something is to _____**possess** it. When people have their things taken away, they are _____**possessed**.
arrange: to put things in a certain order	To put things in order again is to _____**arrange** them. If things are out of order, they are _____**arranged**. If you arrange things in advance, you _____**arrange** them.

Often a prefix comes before a word root. The root cannot stand alone.

con- means together or with	To <u>con</u>struct is to build by putting pieces *together*.

Below are some words you have studied that have the prefix *con-*.

WORD AND MEANING	WRITE HOW THE PREFIX AFFECTS THE MEANING
conclude: to come to a decision or to finish	When you **conclude**, you bring all the parts of something _____.
consultation: a meeting to ask for or to get advice	If you have a **consultation** with someone, you meet _____ that person.

→ YOUR TURN

Choose the right word

> conclude   consultation   rearrange
> prearrange   disarranged   discontinue

Fill each blank with the correct word from the box.

1. We asked for a _____ with the guidance counselor to decide which courses to take.

2. Mac _____ the puzzle pieces by scattering them around.

3. Everyone should _____ a meeting place in case of a fire.

4. It took hours to _____ the furniture after the school party.

5. We were told to _____ riding our bikes on the sidewalk.

6. Be sure to _____ your essay with your strongest point.

Choose the prefix

> re- dis- pre-

Add the correct prefix to the word in parentheses. Write the word.

7. (arranged) After the class trip, we all met at a place that had been _____ by the teachers.

8. (possess) My aunt's job is to _____ cars that haven't been paid for and return them to the dealer.

9. (continues) Whenever I find a shirt I really like, the maker _____ it, and I can't buy it anymore.

10. (arrange) After my little sister uses my markers, I have to _____ them.

11. (arranges) Mia _____ all my stuff and I find things in strange places.

12. (possessed) After the flood destroyed their homes, we sent clothes to the people who were _____.

Show that you know

Complete the sentences.

> Show that you know the words by writing about traveling back in time.

13. If I could travel to the past, I would try to have a *consultation* with _____

14. Another thing I would do if I could go back in time is *repossess* _____

READ on your OWN
Strange Journeys, pages 23–25

BEFORE YOU READ

Think about what you read in Chapter 6. What did the four friends learn about the asteroid?

AS YOU READ

Read "Ask an Expert," pages 23–25.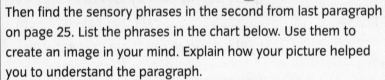
Then find the sensory phrases in the second from last paragraph on page 25. List the phrases in the chart below. Use them to create an image in your mind. Explain how your picture helped you to understand the paragraph.

VOCABULARY

Watch for the words you are learning about.

consulting: seeking information or advice

consultation: a meeting in which information is given

input: data or ideas that are added or offered

revision: a change, usually for the better

revising: changing, usually to improve

FLUENCY

Read sentences that end with an exclamation point in an excited or surprised tone of voice.

Sensory phrases	How my picture helped me understand

AFTER YOU READ

Suppose you traveled into the future and couldn't return to the present. What aspects of your present life would you miss the most?

VISUALIZE: Draw Conclusions

How to Visualize

Use pictures to help you visualize what the passage does and does not tell you.	**Find descriptive and sensory words** and use them to form pictures in your mind of what you are reading.	**Draw conclusions** after forming pictures in your mind about what you are reading.	**Visualize a sequence** of events to help you understand what you are reading.	**Use visual aids,** such as graphic organizers, to help you understand what you are reading.

Learn the STRATEGY

You can use pictures you create in your mind and what you know from personal experience to draw conclusions about what you read. Read the scene below. Then create a picture in your mind of the scene.

> The long, tough football game between Monroe School and Oakwood School was finally over. The Monroe team hurried off the field. The players glowed with pride and happiness.

The paragraph does not state who won, but you can use your mental picture and what you know about athletic games to draw a likely conclusion—the Monroe team won the game.

Read the passage below.

THE TUNGUSKA VALLEY MYSTERY

It was June 30, 1908. The early morning sun hung low in the sky as the train snaked east across Siberia. The sleepy passengers stared out the train windows.

Suddenly, a deafening boom shook the train. The train engineer brought the train to a sudden, screeching halt. The dazed and wide-eyed passengers saw a rocket-shaped object brighter than the sun zooming north. Then the low-flying, blazing object exploded over the Tunguska Valley. Passengers saw a mushroom-shaped cloud billow skyward. They stared out the train windows, white-faced and stunned.

Use the details in the passage and what you know from personal experience to create a mental image of the train passengers. Then circle the letter of a conclusion below that you think is the most reasonable one to draw.

a. The passengers were bored by the fiery object and unconcerned about the explosion.

b. The passengers were startled by the fiery object and frightened by the explosion.

c. The passengers were happy to see the fiery object but annoyed by the explosion.

YOUR TURN

Read "What Was It?" Look for details that help you to draw conclusions about the passage.

What Was It?

1. Reread the first paragraph. What details are given about the Tunguska Valley?

2. Use the details given about the Tunguska Valley disaster to create a mental picture of the scene. Circle a letter of a conclusion below that you think is the most reasonable one to draw.
   a. No one died because there was very little destruction in the area.
   b. Many people died because the area was a popular tourist spot.
   c. No one died because so few people lived in the remote and unhealthy area.

Nearly a century after the event, we still don't know for sure what exploded in Siberia's Tunguska Valley. There were very few witnesses. The valley is very remote, or out of the way, and scarcely populated. Scientists didn't explore the site until almost 20 years after the explosion. The area is difficult to get to and full of swamps and mosquitoes.

The first scientist to explore the valley expected to find a meteorite the size of a house. He also expected to find a hole in the ground as large as the Grand Canyon. He had to **revise** his theory when he found neither. There was some **consolation** in what he did find, however. For as far as he could see, pine trees had been blown down like so many flimsy matchsticks. The damaged area was more than half the size of Rhode Island, but no loss of human life occurred.

Scientists have consulted one another on many occasions to discuss what happened. They have considered **input** of many sorts. Some people have put forth strange explanations for the blast, including a nuclear-powered spaceship from another planet. The likeliest explanation, however, is that a small comet exploded above the area. Knowing what caused the explosion might be helpful in the future. It would allow people to take **suitable** steps to protect life and property from comets that might strike Earth in the future.

Change the expression in your voice to reflect whether information is surprising, serious, or descriptive.

FLUENCY

READ on your OWN
Strange Journeys, pages 26–28

BEFORE YOU READ

Think about what you read in Chapter 7. How do the four friends get the time machine to work again?

AS YOU READ

Read "Exit Finton Fenton," pages 26–28.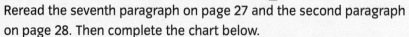
Reread the seventh paragraph on page 27 and the second paragraph on page 28. Then complete the chart below.

VOCABULARY
Watch for the words you are learning about.

filtered: partly passed through

consolation: something that comforts someone

suitably: in a proper way

console: to comfort

suitable: fitting or proper

FLUENCY
Read quotations with a different tone than you use to read the rest of the text.

DETAILS ABOUT MARISSA'S BEHAVIOR	→	MY PERSONAL EXPERIENCE	→	MY CONCLUSION

AFTER YOU READ

Choose the most interesting character or event from this chapter. Describe the character or event.

VISUALIZE: Sequence of Events

How to Visualize

Use pictures to help you visualize what the passage does and does not tell you.	**Find descriptive and sensory words** and use them to form pictures in your mind of what you are reading.	**Draw conclusions** after forming pictures in your mind about what you are reading.	**Visualize a sequence** of events to help you understand what you are reading.	**Use visual aids,** such as graphic organizers, to help you understand what you are reading.

Learn the STRATEGY

When we talk about a trip we took, we often describe events in the order in which they took place. In other words, we use the sequence of events to describe our trip. Good readers visualize the sequence of events in a passage. This helps them remember and understand what they are reading. They use clue words such as *first*, *next*, *after*, *then*, and *finally* to keep track of the order of events. Then they create a mental picture of each event, one after another.

Read the passage below.

A NEW KIND OF STAR

In 1967, an astronomy student named Jocelyn Bell-Burnell, her professor, and a group of fellow students discovered a new kind of star. Here's what happened.

First, the group observed an unusual radio signal. It seemed to be coming from the Milky Way Galaxy. Next, the group investigated possible sources on Earth for the signal. They were not able to find a source that would account for the signal, however. Then, Bell-Burnell discovered another pulsing signal coming from the opposite side of the galaxy. Bell-Burnell and her fellow astronomers realized that the two signals must be from a new kind of star. Finally, in 1968, scientists decided that the signals were from pulsars. Pulsars are stars that form when massive stars die.

Underline the words in the second paragraph of the passage that are clues to the sequence of events.

Number the events below in the order in which they took place.

____ Bell-Burnell found another pulsing signal.

____ The group found that the signal was not coming from sources on Earth.

____ Scientists decided that the signal was from a new kind of star.

____ Bell-Burnell and other astronomers found a new, pulsing radio signal.

Read "Tracking Comets." Then reread the passage and think about the sequence of events in the third, fourth, and fifth paragraphs.

SCIENCE CONNECTION

Tracking Comets

Have you ever seen a comet through a telescope? When seen through a telescope, a comet looks like a small, faint star in a hazy cloud. Comets have a solid core that contains ice and dust particles. When a comet moves close to the Sun, ice in the core vaporizes. The vaporized ice forms a "cloud" of gases and dust. The craters we see on the Moon were caused by the impact of comets.

Astronomers find comets pretty fascinating. Perhaps that's why an astronomer named Carolyn Shoemaker has studied them for so long. In fact, she has discovered 32 comets over the years!

In 1994, Shoemaker was studying an unusual comet. First, she noticed that the comet looked squashed. Later, she **concluded** that the comet was actually made up of 21 fragments, or pieces. Then, she learned that the comet was going to hit the planet Jupiter. She was excited. No one had ever seen a comet hit a planet in our solar system.

Finally, on July 16, 1994, she saw 16 fragments hit Jupiter, one after another. Shoemaker concluded that there was a huge amount of soot, or carbonlike material, in the fragments. What would have happened if the fragments had hit Earth? Shoemaker **theorized** that the soot would have covered our planet in less than 90 minutes.

The comet (at the bottom) on its collision course with Jupiter

Underline the words in the third, fourth, and fifth paragraphs that are clues to the sequence of events.

Number the events below in the order in which they took place.

____ Shoemaker saw 16 fragments hit Jupiter.

____ Shoemaker noticed that the comet looked squashed.

____ Shoemaker learned that the comet was going to hit Jupiter.

____ Shoemaker concluded that the comet was made up of 21 fragments.

When reading, show expression in your voice by letting it rise at the end of a question.

FLUENCY

READ on your OWN
Strange Journeys, pages 29–31

BEFORE YOU READ

Think about what you read in Chapter 8. What does Finton Fenton tell the four friends about traveling to the future again?

AS YOU READ

Read "One Last Trip," pages 29–31.
Then create a picture in your mind of the sequence of events described on page 29. Complete the chart below by numbering the five events in the order in which they occurred.

Events described on page 29	Order of events
They activate the machine and travel into the future.	
Once inside the time machine, they set the time for 2605.	
The four friends decide to return to the future.	
A man with orange eyes greets them.	
They find themselves in a restaurant where people are dancing.	

AFTER YOU READ

Would you want to live on the greatly improved Earth described by Agent Andrew-5? Why?

VOCABULARY
Watch for the words you are learning about.

console: to comfort

input: data that is put in or added

revise: to change, usually to improve

FLUENCY
This story creates strong feelings. Let your expression and tone of voice reflect what each character is feeling.

Make Words Yours!

Learn the WORDS

Here are some words you will be reading. They are also words you need to know for your everyday reading.

WORD AND EXPLANATION	EXAMPLE	WRITE AN EXAMPLE
Something that is **elaborate** is complicated or has a lot of detail.	The bride's dress had **elaborate** beadwork on it.	When have you given an **elaborate** description of something?
To **qualify** is to complete what is needed to do something, like enter a competition.	I hope I **qualify** to compete in the swimming meet.	What do you need to **qualify** for a job?
If you go on a **quest**, you are on a long search for something.	Gavin called the Humane Society in his **quest** for his lost dog.	What kind of **quest** have you been on?
To **quote** someone is to restate his or her exact words.	We need to **quote** sources to support our position.	Who might a reporter **quote** in an article about a basketball game?
Something is **radical** if it is very drastic or extreme.	Gina felt **radical** when she dyed her hair purple.	What is a **radical** idea?
When you have a **surplus**, you have more than the amount that you need.	Jon has a **surplus** of house paint, so he's painting the garage, too.	What would you like to have a **surplus** of?
Toiling is doing very hard, usually physical, work.	Brent and Jayna are **toiling** in the kitchen, scrubbing pots and pans.	What is your least favorite thing to be **toiling** at?
If you are **unfit** for something, you are in poor shape or condition for it.	Sam is **unfit** to be a lifeguard because he can't even swim across the pool.	What is something a child is **unfit** to do?

YOUR TURN

Answer these questions and be ready to explain your answers.

1. Does a rabbit *qualify* as a pet?
   _____

2. Is it *radical* to think that school should last all year? _____

3. Is working on a science project *toiling*?
   _____

4. Can you *quote* a poem?
   _____

Choose the right word

> elaborate   qualify   quest   quote
> radical   surplus   toiling   unfit

Fill each blank with the correct word.

5. We're on a _____ to find the oldest book in the library.

6. The _____ of canned goods was given to the food bank.

7. Rick is _____ to be an astronaut because he is afraid to fly.

8. I have been _____ all day cleaning my room.

9. My uncle belonged to a _____ student group when he was in college.

10. Did you _____ your source or put it in your own words?

11. My bike didn't _____ for the competition because of its tires.

12. Jess has _____ handwriting with all kinds of loops and swirls.

Imagine a weird place. Use the words to describe it.

Show that you know

Use each word below in a sentence.

13. *quest*

_____

_____

_____

14. *elaborate*

_____

_____

_____

15. *surplus*

_____

_____

_____

16. *unfit*

_____

_____

_____

READ on your OWN
Strange Journeys, pages 32–36

BEFORE YOU READ

Think about a weird place you have visited or heard about. What do you think makes a place weird?

AS YOU READ

Read pages 32–36.
The selection "Weird Places" tells about a tour of unusual places. Fill in the chart below. The numbers on the left show the order of the stops on the tour. Write in the names of the places in the boxes on the right.

Stops on the tour	Weird places to visit
1	
2	
3	
4	
5	

VOCABULARY
Watch for the words you are learning about.

surplus: more than the amount that is needed

elaborately: done with a lot of detail

quest: a search for something

radical: very different

FLUENCY
Change the expression in your voice to reflect whether information is surprising, serious, or descriptive.

AFTER YOU READ

Choose a page and tell the most interesting thing you read about on that page.

VISUALIZE: Steps in a Process

How to Visualize

Use pictures to help you visualize what the passage does and does not tell you.

Find descriptive and sensory words and use them to form pictures in your mind of what you are reading.

Draw conclusions after forming pictures in your mind about what you are reading.

Visualize a sequence of events to help you understand what you are reading.

Use visual aids, such as graphic organizers, to help you understand what you are reading.

Learn the STRATEGY

Have you ever followed a recipe or made a craft project? If so, you know that books sometimes have information about how to perform an activity or make something. Good readers know that it is important to stop and think about the steps in a process. Then they can be sure they understand the steps as they read. When reading the steps in a process, certain words are clues to the order of the steps. Words like *first, next, then*, and *finally* help readers understand what they are reading.

Ramon practiced yoga by watching a hologram of a yoga master. Ramon carefully imitated every move the hologram made.

First, Ramon stood straight with his shoulders back and his arms by his sides. Next, Ramon spread his feet wide apart. He turned his right foot so that his toes were pointing away to the side and kept the toes of his left foot pointing forward. Then, he bent his left knee. The main part of his body stayed facing forward.

Next, Ramon lifted his arms straight out on either side of his body so that they were level with his shoulders. Ramon looked down his right arm. Then, he checked the hologram to make sure that his form was correct. It wasn't. Finally, he straightened his fingers and turned his arm so his palm was toward the floor. Perfect!

Which words in the passage are clues to the order of the steps that Ramon followed? Circle the words that are clues.

a. next
b. finally
c. first
d. pointing
e. then
f. palm

Read the passage again. This time, picture the steps in your mind as you read. Visualize Ramon as he does each step in the yoga pose.

How did making a movie in your mind help you understand the passage?

_____

_____

_____

VISUALIZE: Seeing the Big Picture

How to Visualize

Use pictures to help you visualize what the passage does and does not tell you.

Find descriptive and sensory words and use them to form pictures in your mind of what you are reading.

Draw conclusions after forming pictures in your mind about what you are reading.

Visualize a sequence of events to help you understand what you are reading.

Use visual aids, such as graphic organizers, to help you understand what you are reading.

Learn the STRATEGY

You have learned how visualizing information can help you better understand what you read. When you form pictures in your mind of what you are reading, it helps you to remember what you have read. Creating graphic organizers helps you to organize the information you have read. Then you can understand it better.

A FIELD OF CORN

Imagine a field filled with 109 upright ears of corn. That's what visitors to Dublin, Ohio, can see along the highway that runs through town. Each ear is about 6 feet tall. The people-sized ears are made of concrete. The ears stand like soldiers at attention in a parade.

An artist created this unusual art display in 1994. The Field of Corn was built on land that was once owned by Sam Frantz. Frantz worked at growing new and different types of corn. When Frantz's farming days were over, he donated his farm to make a park. Many people from Dublin think the 6-foot-tall ears of concrete corn are just plain corny!

Which descriptive words best help you form pictures in your mind as you read?

a. 6-foot-tall ears of concrete corn
b. land that was once owned
c. 109 upright ears of corn
d. stand like soldiers at attention

Write the words from this passage that give you the best picture in your mind.

_____
_____
_____
_____

YOUR TURN

Read "Field of Dreams." Think about which graphic organizer will help you understand the passage.

1. Which graphic organizer will be the best one to use to help you visualize the information in the passage?
- **a.** flowchart
- **b.** idea web
- **c.** timeline

2. Explain why you picked the graphic organizer you did.

3. Use the space below to draw and fill in a graphic organizer, such as an idea web.

FIELD OF DREAMS

In 1989 a popular movie was *Field of Dreams*. It showed a baseball diamond in a cornfield. At the movie's end, **looming** ghosts of long-dead baseball players ran out through the corn. The ghosts played a game with the movie's star. Imagine that someone told you this had actually happened. Would you think it was just a **hoax** to get you to visit the baseball field? Or would you want to visit the field anyway because you enjoyed the movie?

A quarter of a century after the movie came out, the actual Field of Dreams is still popular. It is on its way to becoming a famous tourist attraction. The baseball field in the movie was constructed in an **obscure** cornfield near Dyersville, Iowa. More than 50,000 people visit it each year. Visitors can watch a local team wearing old-fashioned baseball uniforms play a game. If they want to, visitors can play baseball, run around the bases, take pictures, or buy snacks and baseball **relics** at one of the gift shops. Half of the Field of Dreams is located on one farm, and the other half is located on another. Things get confusing in the evening, though. One family closes its side of the field at 6 p.m., **whereas** the other family keeps its side open until sunset. So after six, you can only play on half the field!

Vary your expression to make your reading sound smoother and more interesting.

FLUENCY

READ on your OWN
Strange Journeys, pages 59–61

BEFORE YOU READ

Think about the last pages you read in "Weird Places." Did everyone agree about whether the metal pieces that Brazel found were from a flying saucer?

AS YOU READ

Read pages 59–61.
Use the idea web below to organize the important details about the UFO Museum. In each box, write in something that visitors to the museum can see.

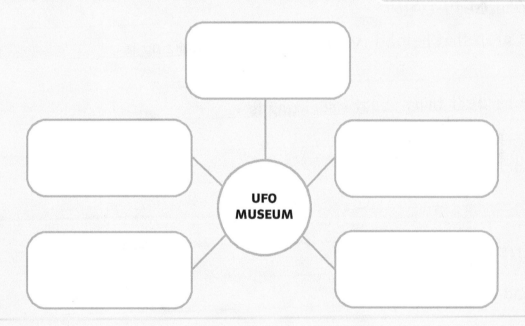

UFO MUSEUM

AFTER YOU READ

Do you think that UFOs are real? Why or why not?

Unit 5 Reflection

VOCABULARY

The easiest part of learning new words is

The hardest part is

I still need to work on

Strange Journeys

COMPREHENSION

The step that helped me the most with visualizing is

The hardest thing about visualizing is

I still need to work on

FLUENCY

I read most fluently when

I still need to work on

INDEPENDENT READING

My favorite part of Strange Journeys is

Nature in the EXTREME

COMPREHENSION
LEARN HOW TO INFER—THINK BEYOND THE TEXT

INDEPENDENT READING
Nature in the Extreme
Includes "Volcanic Eruptions" and "San Francisco Shaking!"

unit 6

VOCABULARY

WORDS:
Know them!
Use them in reading and writing!
Learn what they mean!

FLUENCY
Make your reading smooth and accurate, one tip at a time.

Make Words Yours!

Learn the WORDS

Here are some words you will be reading in the next week.
They will also help you in your everyday reading.

WORD AND EXPLANATION	EXAMPLE	WRITE AN EXAMPLE
If you are a **bystander**, you watch an activity without taking part in it.	The firefighters asked the **bystander** to move out of the way.	When have you been a **bystander**?
To **decrease** means to become less or smaller. It also means to make something less or smaller.	Tanya asked her boss to **decrease** her work hours.	What else might you want to **decrease**?
A **dwelling** is a house or place where people live.	A tepee is a kind of Native American **dwelling**.	What is another example of a **dwelling**?
When you **enlarge** something, you make it bigger.	I will **enlarge** the photo before I frame it.	How can you **enlarge** a CD collection?
A **formation** is something that is made or develops into a particular shape. The **formation** of something is the beginning or development of it.	The rock **formation** was caused by volcanic activity.	What is another natural **formation**?
The **frequency** of something is how often it repeats, or happens again and again.	Lightning increases the **frequency** of forest fires.	What is something you do with great **frequency**?
A **portion** of something is a part of it.	The fire damaged one **portion** of the home.	What **portion** of the day do you spend sleeping?
A **vicinity** is an area around something.	There is only one movie theater in our **vicinity**.	What is something you can find in the **vicinity** of your home?

➤ YOUR TURN

Choose the right word

bystander	decrease	dwelling	enlarge
formation	frequency	portion	vicinity

Fill each blank with the correct word from the box.

1. The _____ left the accident scene to call an ambulance.

2. During snow storms, the _____ of car accidents increases.

3. We will have to _____ the print so everyone can read it easily.

4. Black bears live in this general _____.

5. It's not fair if some kids get a larger _____ of cake.

6. The students want to discuss the _____ of a drama club.

7. The tornado totally destroyed the _____.

8. The dry weather will _____ the size of our tomato crop.

Understand the words

Circle the best answer to each question.

9. When something *enlarges*, which does it become? **bigger** or **smaller**

10. Which can be a *dwelling*? **cabin** or **field**

11. Which describes something in your *vicinity*? **far** or **near**

12. Which happens with less *frequency* in deserts? **sunshine** or **rain**

13. When things *decrease*, what do they become? **larger** or **smaller**

14. Which is an example of a *portion*? **whole** or **half**

> Show that you know the words by writing about events in nature.

Show that you know

Complete the sentences.

15. Dark cloud *formations* might mean _____

16. During accidents and natural disasters, *bystanders* should _____

READ on your OWN
Nature in the Extreme, pages 3–5

BEFORE YOU READ

Think about what you already know about volcanoes. How can volcanoes be dangerous to people?

AS YOU READ

Read pages 3–4 of "The Fury of Volcanoes." (STOP)
Answer the questions below.

Why do you think so many people in Pompeii were unable to escape the eruption of Mt. Vesuvius and were buried by ash? _____

_____

_____

From what you read and what you already know, why are volcanoes life-threatening? _____

_____

_____

Read "The Birth of a Volcano," page 5. (STOP)
Answer the question below.

Do you think it is possible to prevent a volcano from erupting? Why or why not? _____

_____

_____

AFTER YOU READ

Would you be willing to live near a volcano? Why or why not?

VOCABULARY
Watch for the words you are learning about.

formation: shape

portion: part

enlarge: increase in size

vicinity: surrounding area

FLUENCY
To read more smoothly, preview the text and decide ahead of time where to pause.

INFER: Figure Out the Meaning

How to Infer

Use **what you know**. Combine your experience with what you learned and what you read.	Use information about people, places, and events in **fiction** and **nonfiction**.	Use information to **predict** what will happen next in the text.	Identify the **causes**, or what made something happen, and the **effects**, or what happened.	Distinguish between those statements that are **facts** and those statements that are **opinions**.

Learn the STRATEGY

Inferring means using what you know to figure out a meaning not directly stated in something you hear or read. Good readers make inferences all the time. They know that inferring helps them understand and remember what they read. To make an inference, put what you read together with what you know.

(WHAT YOU READ) ➕ (WHAT YOU KNOW) 🟰 (INFERENCE)

You make inferences all the time. For example, if you see dark clouds in the sky, you might infer that it will rain. You know from past experience that when dark clouds appear in the sky, it usually rains.

Think about the reaction of each boy in the cartoon below to what the newscaster is saying.

The erupting volcano sent ashes and a huge black cloud of dust and other debris into the air.

That volcano was near a big town. I bet a lot of homes were destroyed.

I remember when Mount St. Helens erupted. We saw videos of it in school. It was awesome!

Which boy in the picture is making an inference?
a. the boy in the baseball cap
b. the boy with the drink can
c. both boys

What does this boy already know about volcanoes?

a. Erupting volcanoes can be very destructive.
b. Erupting volcanoes are always near big towns.
c. Erupting volcanoes are awesome sights.

What is his inference?

a. Videos are a good way to see erupting volcanoes.
b. Erupting volcanoes send ash and dust into the air.
c. Erupting volcanoes near towns can destroy homes.

YOUR TURN

Read "A Warning!" Then answer the numbered questions.

1. Wafulah receives no salary for his work. You know that people must earn a living to survive. What can you infer about Wafulah based on what you know and the text?
  a. Wafulah is rich.
  b. Wafulah must really love to study volcanoes.
  c. Wafulah is wasting his time studying volcanoes.

2. What does Wafulah already know about volcanoes?

3. Was there a time when you warned someone about something that wasn't acted on and should have been? Use this memory to infer how Wafulah might have felt about his warnings being ignored.

A Warning!

Dieudonne Wafulah (DEE-yoo-duhn WAH-foo-lah) is a volcanologist—a scientist who studies volcanoes. For years, he has studied volcanoes in the Democratic Republic of Congo. Wafulah is the only volcanologist in his country and receives no salary for his efforts. He depends entirely on donations from foreigners.

In 2000, a small mountain that Wafulah had been observing erupted. The volcanologist was convinced that nearby Mount Nyiragongo (nyee-rah-GAWNG-goh) would erupt next. For 2 years, he observed the larger **formation** carefully. He noticed that the number of earthquakes increased and that the volcano's crater changed shape and **enlarged**.

On January 8, 2002, Wafulah sent an urgent e-mail to the authorities warning of an eruption. However, the authorities didn't consider the volcano dangerous. They believed that **bystanders** could easily avoid any lava flows.

On January 17, the volcano erupted and lava began flowing toward the city of Goma, 12 miles away. The molten lava rapidly buried trees, highways, and **dwellings**. A day later, 40 percent of the city was destroyed. About 100 people were thought to have died.

The city of Goma cleans up after the eruption.

Dieudonne Wafulah says he will continue to study volcanoes. In fact, he is considering moving to Goma to be closer to the danger zone.

Practice pausing at periods when you read. FLUENCY

READ on your OWN
Nature in the Extreme, pages 7–9

BEFORE YOU READ

Think about the last pages you read in "Volcanic Eruptions." How can a volcanic eruption affect an area thousands of miles away?

AS YOU READ

Read pages 7–8 of "When Plates Collide."
In the chart below, write something you already know and make an inference to answer the question.

Read "Types of Volcanoes," page 9.
Write something you know and your inference in the chart.

When Plates Collide	Types of Volcanoes
Question What formed the Hawaiian Islands?	**Question** Why are shield volcanoes less dangerous than caldera volcanoes?
What I know	**What I know**
My inference	**My inference**

AFTER YOU READ

What would interest you most about visiting an area where there are active volcanoes?

VOCABULARY
Watch for the words you are learning about.

frequency: number of times a thing happens

dwelling: living

bystanders: people who are near an event but are not part of it

FLUENCY
Practice pausing at each period.

Get Wordwise!
Recognizing Shades of Meaning

Learn More About the WORDS

Small differences in meaning can make one word better to use than another. The words *walk* and *stroll* are similar in meaning. However, a stroll is a slow, casual walk. A person walking fast would not be strolling. The two words have different **shades of meaning**.

WORD AND EXPLANATION	WORD IN SENTENCE	CIRCLE THE BETTER WORD
To **decrease** means to become or make less or smaller.	Tim's parents said they will **decrease** his allowance.	Which can **decrease**? **temperature** or **gravity**
To **diminish** means to gradually become less or smaller.	The rain will **diminish** by noon.	Which **diminishes**? **a window** or **an ice cube in the sun**
To **enlarge** means to make bigger in size.	The teacher will **enlarge** the map so everyone can see it.	Which can be **enlarged**? **a parachute** or **a book collection**
To **inflate** means to make larger by adding air.	Bob will **inflate** the balloons.	Which can be **inflated**? **a rubber raft** or **a photograph**
A **dwelling** is a house or place where people live.	Some animals use trees as their **dwellings**.	Which is a **dwelling**? **a store** or **an apartment**
A **shelter** is a place that provides protection.	We brought the stray dog to an animal **shelter**.	Which can be a **shelter**? **a cave** or **a lock**
A **vicinity** is an area around something.	There are few houses in the **vicinity** of the power plant.	Which is more likely to be found in the **vicinity** of a warehouse? **a vegetable garden** or **a parking lot**
A **neighborhood** is an area of homes.	The boys grew up in the same **neighborhood**.	Which makes up a **neighborhood**? **a junkyard** or **a housing development**

YOUR TURN

Decide whether each statement is true or false. Be ready to explain your answers.

1. If you withdraw money from the bank, your balance will *decrease*. _____

2. People who live close to one another live in the same *vicinity*. _____

3. If you *enlarge* a photograph, you make it smaller. _____

4. If a building provides *shelter*, it is a *dwelling*. _____

Choose the right word

> decrease diminish   dwelling
> shelter   neighborhood inflate

Fill each blank with the word from the box with the shade of meaning that best fits the sentence.

5. The price will _____ when the records go on sale.

6. The tent was our _____ for the night.

7. There are a lot of trees in my friend's _____.

8. The sound will gradually _____ until you can't hear it at all.

9. To fix a flat tire, you need to _____ it.

10. A town house is a type of _____ that some people live in.

Show that you know shades of meaning by writing about nature.

Show that you know

Complete the sentences.

11. When clouds thicken and *enlarge*

12. If I saw clouds *diminish*, I might think

13. If my home were in the *vicinity* of a volcano,

14. During a flood, *neighborhoods* can

READ on your OWN
Nature in the Extreme, pages 10–12

BEFORE YOU READ

Think about the last pages you read in "Volcanic Eruptions." How can a volcano create an island?

AS YOU READ

Read page 10 of "Ancient Eruptions."
In the chart below, write something you already know and make an inference to answer the question.

Read page 11.
Write something you know and your inference in the chart.

Read page 12.
Write something you know and your inference in the chart.

Page 10	Page 11	Page 12
Question Why is a volcanic eruption in the future a real possibility in the Yellowstone area?	**Question** What does the presence of so many hydrothermal features tell you about Yellowstone?	**Question** Why would an eruption at Yellowstone now be more disastrous than the eruptions of 600,000 years ago?
What I know	**What I know**	**What I know**
My inference	**My inference**	**My inference**

VOCABULARY
Watch for the words you are learning about.

portion(s): section(s) of a larger whole

bystanders: people who are near an event but are not caught up in it

formations: land features

frequency: high rate of occurrence

FLUENCY
To improve your reading, practice pausing at periods.

AFTER YOU READ

Do you think it would be dangerous to live near Yellowstone? Why or why not?

INFER: Use Personal Experience

How to Infer

Use **what you know**. Combine your experience with what you learned and what you read.

Use information about people, places, and events in **fiction** and **nonfiction**.

Use information to **predict** what will happen next in the text.

Identify the **causes**, or what made something happen, and the **effects**, or what happened.

Distinguish between those statements that are **facts** and those statements that are **opinions**.

Learn the STRATEGY

Often in school, you are asked to tell about or answer questions that are in the text. Sometimes you are asked questions that go "beyond the text." For these, you will need to rely on personal experience to make an inference that can answer the question.

Many beyond-the-text questions involve making an inference. Use something that you know about the subject from personal experience. Questions that ask you to make an inference help you think about the many things you already know. They also help you remember what you read.

It says here that Mount Etna in Italy is the largest volcano in Europe and is a constant threat to the people that live on its slopes. However, the volcano's eruptions have also made the soil there very fertile. Plus, the warm climate is perfect for growing fruit.

My cousins live in California, even though there is a constant threat of earthquakes there. I guess people will live wherever the climate is nice and they can earn a living, even if there are dangers.

What inference can be made based on the cartoon and the girl's experience?

a. The climate is nice in Italy and different fruits are grown there.

b. People in California also grow fruit.

c. People will risk living in danger zones as long as there are benefits to living there.

What experience did the girl rely on to make this inference?

a. She has experienced an earthquake herself.

b. She has cousins who live in California and may know something about what grows there.

c. She has visited Italy.

YOUR TURN

"The God of Fire" is a personal account of someone who lived near Mount Etna in ancient times. Read it and then follow the numbered directions.

The God of Fire

1. Circle an inference the storyteller is making.
   a. The mountain is rumbling and spurting smoke and fire again.
   b. Vulcan and his helpers must be hard at work in their workshop beneath Mount Etna.
   c. Jupiter is the head of all the Roman gods.

2. What inference can you make about the storyteller taking fish to the god Vulcan?
   a. He thinks it will calm the god's anger.
   b. He thinks the fish will help him pray better.
   c. He wants to visit with the people who are building fires along the banks of the river.

The mountain is rumbling and spurting smoke and fire again today. I have even felt the ground shake in this **vicinity**, several miles from the volcano. Vulcan and his helpers must be hard at work in their workshop beneath Mount Etna. Perhaps they are making thunderbolts for Jupiter, the head of all the Roman gods. Of course, they may be creating new weapons for Mars, the god of war, instead.

For a time, the rumblings had **decreased** and things were quiet and peaceful. Now the mountain seems to shake with greater **frequency** each day. Some people fear that Vulcan is angry. I do not know if this is so. However, tomorrow I will go to visit the temple of the god Vulcan. People are building fires there along the banks of the river. Like others, I will bring fish as my **portion** of the offering to Vulcan. I will pray that the fire god will protect our town from harm this time.

3. What do you think the storyteller fears is likely to happen soon?

4. Based on personal experience, do you think using fish for a sacrifice will help prevent a volcanic eruption?

To read aloud more smoothly, practice pausing at commas.

FLUENCY

READ on your OWN
Nature in the Extreme, pages 13–15

BEFORE YOU READ

Think about the last pages you read in "Volcanic Eruptions." Why do scientists consider Yellowstone a "living laboratory"?

AS YOU READ

Read "Taken by Surprise," page 13.
In the chart below, write something you already know and make an inference to answer the question.

Read "Unearthing Pompeii," pages 14–15.
Write something you know and your inference in the chart.

Taken by Surprise	Unearthing Pompeii
Question Why didn't the people who lived near Mount Vesuvius leave before it erupted?	**Question** Why didn't people dig up Pompeii before the 1700s?
What I know	**What I know**
My inference	**My inference**

VOCABULARY
Watch for the words you are learning about.

bystander: person who is near an event but is not caught up in it

vicinity: area around a place

decrease: lessen

dwellings: homes

portions: sections of a larger whole

FLUENCY
Remember to pause when you come to a comma or a period.

AFTER YOU READ

What do you think your response would be to seeing the "frozen" remains of a victim of Pompeii?

Make Words Yours!

Learn the WORDS

Here are some words you will be reading in the next week. They are also words you need to know for your everyday reading.

WORDS AND EXPLANATION	EXAMPLE	WRITE AN EXAMPLE
Debris is the remains of something that has been destroyed.	The firefighters cleared away the **debris** after the fire died down.	What is an event that can leave **debris** behind?
When you **heed** something, you pay attention to it.	We **heeded** the warnings and stayed away from the edge of the cliff.	What warnings have you **heeded**?
Something that is **moderate** is mild, not great or extreme.	After the hot summer, I appreciate the **moderate** weather of fall.	What illnesses can be **moderate**?
To **refresh** is to make something or someone feel stronger, more energetic, or almost like new.	A good night's sleep will **refresh** you.	What is something else that can **refresh** you?
To **rely** on is to depend on someone or something.	We **rely** on weather forecasts to plan our weekend.	Who is someone you can **rely** on?
Something that is **secure** is safe from risk or danger.	I feel more **secure** when my doors are locked.	How can you help a young child feel **secure**?
A **technique** is a method or way of doing something.	What **technique** did you use to make the model?	What is a **technique** you have used to do something?
When you **undergo** something, you experience it, but usually would rather not, such as a bad experience or change.	We had to **undergo** a security check before getting on the plane.	What is something you have had to **undergo** recently?

YOUR TURN

Yes or No?

Answer these questions and be ready to explain your answers.

1. Does rain *refresh* a garden? _____

2. Is a hurricane a *moderate* wind? _____

3. Can you *rely* on your best friend? _____

4. Do you like to learn new *techniques*? _____

Choose the right word

> debris   heed   moderate   refresh
> rely   secure   technique   undergo

Fill each blank with the correct word from the box.

5. I will be sure to [_____] Tina's advice to bring a jacket.

6. The boat will be [_____] in the harbor.

7. After the flood, [_____] blocked the main road.

8. My dog had to [_____] some tests at the vet's.

9. After a long walk, a glass of cool water will [_____] you.

10. Tony is practicing a new skating [_____].

11. You don't need a heavy blanket when the temperature is [_____].

12. Maria will [_____] on us to help her find the way.

Use the words to show what you know about the dangers of volcanoes.

Show that you know

Use each word below in a sentence.

13. *secure*

14. *undergo*

15. *heed*

16. *debris*

READ on your OWN
Nature in the Extreme, pages 16–18

VOCABULARY
Watch for the words you are learning about.

undergo: experience

heeded: listened to

debris: pieces of something that has been destroyed

refresh: clean

FLUENCY
To make your reading smoother, look for commas and periods to show you where to pause to take breaths.

BEFORE YOU READ

Think about the last pages you read in "Volcanic Eruptions." What can scientists learn by studying the ruins of Pompeii?

AS YOU READ

Read page 16 of "Tambora: Year Without a Summer." (STOP)
In the chart below, write something you already know and make an inference to answer the question.

Read page 17. (STOP)
Write something you know and an inference in the chart.

Read page 18. (STOP)
Write something you know and an inference in the chart.

Page 16	Page 17	Page 18
Question Why was food scarce in parts of the world during the summer of 1816?	**Question** Why didn't people leave Sumbawa when the earthquakes started?	**Question** Why did so few people on the island of Sumbawa survive the eruption?
What I know	**What I know**	**What I know**
My inference	**My inference**	**My inference**

AFTER YOU READ

If you had been a survivor of the Tambora eruption, how would you have felt about continuing to live on the island?

INFER:
Use What You Already Know

How to Infer

Use **what you know**. Combine your experience with what you learned and what you read.

Use information about people, places, and events in **fiction** and **nonfiction**.

Use information to **predict** what will happen next in the text.

Identify the **causes**, or what made something happen, and the **effects**, or what happened.

Distinguish between those statements that are **facts** and those statements that are **opinions**.

Learn the STRATEGY

Personal experiences are useful for making inferences, but you don't have to experience a tornado personally to know that it is dangerous. You know many things that are outside the range of your personal experiences.

You know what you learned in school from teachers and textbooks and at home from other family members. You know what you learned from television, magazines, and the Internet. You know what you learned from your friends. All of this knowledge can help you and is very important in making inferences.

In order to understand the following passage, you need to already know some things. Answer the questions in the side column to see how using what you know can help you make inferences.

Circle each of the things in an ecosystem that is nonliving.

a. plants
b. water
c. rocks
d. air
e. animals
f. insects
g. soil

Do you think balance in an ecosystem is a good thing? How can you infer this from what you know about the word *balance*?

_____
_____
_____
_____

Ecosystems are made up of living and nonliving things that are usually in balance with each other. A volcanic eruption may destroy that balance.

Gases with temperatures of more than 1,000 degrees are released into the air. Ash created by the eruption forms thick clouds that can block out sunlight. Huge rocks and boulders are hurled onto the surrounding land, and many living things are killed. Even the soil and water can be damaged. Many years must pass before the ecosystem begins to return to its former state.

Do you think gases with temperatures greater than 1,000 degrees are deadly to living things that breathe them? What do you already know that can help you infer this?

_____
_____
_____
_____

▶ YOUR TURN

Read "A Return to Life." Then follow the numbered directions.

1. You already know that volcanoes can be very destructive. Underline three examples of the destruction in the first paragraph.

2. What can you infer about the trees that were blown down?

3. You have probably heard the word *pioneer*. Using what you know about pioneers, what can you infer about what pioneer plants do?
   a. They are the first plants to grow.
   b. They provide nutrients to the soil.
   c. They can grow on bare rock.

4. What are some other kinds of natural disasters you know about?

5. Make an inference about natural disasters based on what you know and what you read in this passage.

A Return to Life

Mount St. Helens in Washington State erupted on May 18, 1980. Nearly 7,000 land animals died in the blast. Ash, dust, and other **debris** settled into streams and lakes, killing millions of fish. The number of trees blown down by the eruption was enormous. They would have provided enough wood to build 300,000 homes.

For a while, the area's ecosystem was almost empty of life-forms. By 1982, though, life began to return, in a **moderate** way, to the area. Mosses and lichens began growing on bare rock. The rootlike parts of these pioneer plants helped break down the rocks to form soil. As these pioneer plants began to **undergo** the process of decay, they added nutrients to the soil, which helped other plants grow.

Wind and birds deposited seeds in the new soil. The seeds soon sprouted. A few years later, larger plants began to grow. Animals began feeling more **secure** about having a food supply. So they started returning to the area.

By the summer of 1987, much of the area near Mount St. Helens was back to life. The life-forms weren't exactly the same ones that had been there before. This time, flowers such as Indian paintbrush and purple wildflowers dotted the mountain's slopes. However, they were proof that an ecosystem could be destroyed by a volcanic eruption and still return to life.

As you read aloud, vary the loudness and softness of your voice to make the reading sound more natural.

FLUENCY

READ on your OWN
Nature in the Extreme, pages 19–21

BEFORE YOU READ

Think about the last pages you read in "Volcanic Eruptions." Why was it difficult to escape from an island in the 1800s?

AS YOU READ

Read "Snowmen in Summer," pages 19–20.
In the chart below, write something you already know and make an inference to answer the question.

Read "The Legacy of Tambora," page 21.
Write something you know and your inference in the chart.

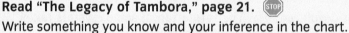

Snowmen in Summer	The Legacy of Tambora
Question How did soot and ash from Tambora spread to other places?	**Question** Why would a new eruption on Sumbawa be more destructive than the 1815 eruption?
What I know	**What I know**
My inference	**My inference**

VOCABULARY
Watch for the words you are learning about.

debris: pieces of something that has been destroyed

moderate: mild

rely: have confidence in

FLUENCY
Remember to pause at the end of each paragraph before continuing to read.

AFTER YOU READ

Which result of the Tambora eruption was most surprising to you?

Get Wordwise!
Words With Multiple Meanings

Learn More About the WORDS

Many words have **more than one meaning**. To know which meaning fits, you need to think about the meaning of the sentence or passage that includes the word.

I used a **pen** to write my report. The pigs are in the **pen**.

The word *pen* can describe a writing tool or an enclosure.

WORD	MEANINGS	WHICH MEANING WORKS?
formation	**a.** something that is made, or developed **b.** the act of making, or shaping **c.** an arrangement of people or things for a purpose	The **formation** of some crystals takes thousands of years. _____ The geese were flying in **formation**. _____
refresh	**a.** to make someone or something stronger, more energetic, or almost new **b.** to awaken or stir up **c.** to update an image on a computer screen	The cold water **refreshed** the runners. _____ If you **refresh** the image on the screen, you will be able to see the most recent pictures. _____
frequency	**a.** something that happens often **b.** how often something happens within a set amount of time **c.** a measure of sound waves or electricity	The **frequency** of birds migrating increases in the autumn. _____ Turn the dial on the radio to find a different **frequency**. _____
secure	**a.** safe from risk or danger **b.** to get **c.** to fasten	She **secured** the two pieces together with a short length of wire. _____ Did you **secure** enough money to pay him back? _____

▶ YOUR TURN

Choose the right word

> formation   frequency   refresh   secure

Fill each blank with the correct word from the box. You will use the words more than once.

1. We need to _____ the railing to the deck.

2. Did hearing the song _____ your memory?

3. The company needs to _____ a lease on the building.

4. What led to the _____ of the book club?

5. The _____ of trains at this stop is one every 15 minutes.

6. Sound waves travel at a different _____ from light waves.

7. A nap will _____ you.

8. The band marched in _____.

9. Global warming means hurricanes can form with greater _____.

10. We climbed to the top of the interesting rock _____.

11. The lid on my hamster's cage keeps him _____.

Yes or No?

Answer these questions and be ready to explain your answers.

12. Would you *refresh* an image if part of it was missing? _____

13. Would washing your face *refresh* you? _____

14. Does looking at photographs *refresh* your memory? _____

15. Does exercising *refresh* you? _____

> Show that you know multiple meanings by writing about forces in nature.

Show that you know

Complete the sentences.

16. To be *secure* during a lightning storm _____

17. During a bad storm, be sure to *secure* _____

18. So that you are not short on supplies, be sure to *secure* _____

READ on your OWN
Nature in the Extreme, pages 22–25

BEFORE YOU READ

Think about the last pages you read in "Volcanic Eruptions."
What made Tambora one of the most destructive eruptions ever?

AS YOU READ

Read pages 22–23 of "Krakatau: The Loudest Volcano Ever."
In the chart below, write something you already know and make
an inference to answer the question.

Read pages 24–25.
Write something you know and your inference in the chart.

Pages 22–23	Pages 24–25
Question Why was Krakatau virtually unknown before 1883?	**Question** Why are scientists interested in Anak Krakatau's growth and earthquakes?
What I know	**What I know**
My inference	**My inference**

AFTER YOU READ

Would you want to visit Anak Krakatau? Why or why not?

VOCABULARY
Watch for the words you are learning about.

technique: method of doing something

secure: free from danger

rely: depend on

FLUENCY
Use breaks in the text to help you read smoothly. Pause at the ends of paragraphs.

INFER: Fiction

How to Infer

Use **what you know**. Combine your experience with what you learned and what you read.	Use information about people, places, and events in **fiction** and **nonfiction**.	Use information to **predict** what will happen next in the text.	Identify the **causes**, or what made something happen, and the **effects**, or what happened.	Distinguish between those statements that are **facts** and those statements that are **opinions**.

Learn the STRATEGY

When you read fiction, you often use your experiences and things you've learned to make inferences about the text. Read the following sentences:

The hot sun beat down on Tina's head. The sand felt scratchy beneath her feet.

What inference can you make about where Tina might be? You might know that many deserts are hot and sandy because you've seen them in movies. Maybe you inferred that Tina was at the beach because you know that beaches are often hot and sandy.

As you have seen, you can make inferences about the places in stories. You can also make inferences about characters in stories and the things that happen to them. To make inferences about characters, think about what the people you know do and say. For example, you know that when people frown, sigh, or roll their eyes, they're usually unhappy. So when a character does any of those things, you can infer that he or she is unhappy.

Read the story below and think about how Maria feels.

"Yes, Mom, I'll take Roberto to the natural history museum," said Maria. She frowned and tried to keep from groaning as she said the words and hung up the phone. Why did her little brother like the Pompeii exhibition so much? Each time they visited it, Roberto's face lit up as he studied the ancient items that were preserved in volcanic ash. "Get your coat, Roberto," she said, forcing a smile. "Guess where we're going?"

Use the story to answer the questions.

What can you infer about how Maria feels about going to the museum?

a. Maria is excited about going.
b. Maria doesn't have any obvious feelings about going.
c. Maria doesn't really want to go.

What words helped you make that inference?

_____

_____

_____

YOUR TURN

Read "A Visit to Norris Geyser Basin." Then answer the numbered questions.

1. At first, how does Tory feel about visiting the geyser basin?

What words helped you make the inference?

2. How does her dad feel about visiting the geyser basin?

What words helped you make the inference?

3. By the end of the story, how does Tory feels about visiting the geyser basin?

What words helped you make the inference?

A Visit to Norris Geyser Basin

Tory trailed behind her father in the museum at Norris Geyser Basin. "Isn't this fantastic?" Dad said, pointing to a display explaining how a geyser worked. Fantastic wasn't the word Tory would use, but one look at her father's beaming face quieted her. Dad loved this stuff, so she'd **undergone** the tour without complaining.

At last they headed outside into the park. "Let's go through Porcelain Basin," Dad suggested. "The ranger said there were lots of geysers within a **moderate** distance."

Tory sighed as she hurried to keep up. Maybe we'll be finished and back to the motel pool by noon, she thought. She was lost in dreams of a **refreshing** swim when she heard her father say, "Wow!"

Tory looked up, her eyes widening. Stretching out before them was a sheet of whitish wet rock, with geysers everywhere, bubbling, gurgling, and popping like mad. It looked like some sort of massive sorcerer's cauldron. "Wow is right," thought Tory as she gazed at the spectacle. She had never seen anything so powerful and impressive and now she knew now why her dad had wanted to come to this place.

"Ready to head back?" Dad asked. Tory shook her head, grabbing the map he held. "We still haven't seen Steamboat Geyser! Come on, Dad, I think it's this way." Dad grinned as he **heeded** her call to catch up.

Use breaks in the text to help you read smoothly. Pause at the ends of paragraphs.

FLUENCY

READ on your OWN
Nature in the Extreme, pages 26–28

BEFORE YOU READ

Think about the last pages you read in "Volcanic Eruptions." Why do scientists continue to monitor Anak Krakatau?

AS YOU READ

Read page 26 of "Mount St. Helens: A Restless Giant." [STOP]
In the chart below, write something you already know and make an inference to answer the question.

Read "The Giant Erupts," pages 27–28. [STOP]
Write something you know and your inference in the chart.

Mount St. Helens: A Restless Giant	*The Giant Erupts*
Question Why did Native Americans tell a story about Mount St. Helens?	**Question** Why did the sky turn dark as night after the eruption of Mount St. Helens?
What I know	**What I know**
My inference	**My inference**

AFTER YOU READ

How would you feel about living near Mount St. Helens? Explain your answer.

INFER: Nonfiction

How to Infer

Use **what you know**. Combine your experience with what you learned and what you read.	Use information about people, places, and events in **fiction** and **nonfiction**.	Use information to **predict** what will happen next in the text.	Identify the **causes**, or what made something happen, and the **effects**, or what happened.	Distinguish between those statements that are **facts** and those statements that are **opinions**.

Learn the STRATEGY

You have learned that good readers infer by using their personal experiences and knowledge. Connecting the text to something you've experienced yourself or learned helps you discover more about the characters, setting, and other aspects of the stories you read.

Did you know that good readers also infer when they read textbooks or other nonfiction text? You can use facts in the text and what you already know to infer ideas that the writer doesn't state directly. Inferring helps a reader better understand nonfiction text.

DEADLY WAVES

More than 36,000 people died when Krakatau, a volcano in Indonesia, erupted in 1883. Few of the victims were killed by flowing lava. Nor were they killed by fumes or burning ash. They were killed by the tsunamis that struck the surrounding islands after the eruption.

I saw a tsunami on the news. It was a huge, strong wave of water. I can infer that the Krakatau tsunamis were so high that many people drowned.

Based on the text, circle the letter of each inference you can make about flowing lava, fumes, and burning ash.

a. Flowing lava, fumes, and burning ash are seen when a volcano erupts.

b. Flowing lava, fumes, and burning ash killed some of the Krakatau victims.

c. The eruption produced a large amount of lava, fumes, and ash.

d. The eruption happened near an ocean or other large body of water.

In the cartoon, the girl reading the passage learned something about tsunamis from the news. What did you already know about the topic? Where did you get the information?

_____

_____

_____

_____

_____

SCIENCE CONNECTION

Tsunamis

A tsunami is a huge wave that forms in deep ocean water. Tsunamis are sometimes called tidal waves.

Causes of Tsunamis For a tsunami to form, a large area of water must move suddenly. This movement can happen when the plates that form the ocean floor collide to cause an earthquake. The ocean floor rises or sinks. As water rushes from the higher section to the lower one, a wave forms.

Landslides often result from earthquakes. Landslides also contribute to the formation of tsunamis. The tons of rock and dirt that fall to the ocean floor push aside large volumes of water.

Undersea volcanoes are another cause of tsunamis. An eruption forces molten rock and gas out of a vent at tremendous speed. This force pushes water away from the area, making a big wave.

Movement of a Tsunami In the deepest parts of the ocean, a tsunami is barely noticeable at the surface. However, as the wave travels toward shallower water, its speed **decreases**. The water starts to pile up and the height of the wave increases. By the time a tsunami reaches land, it can be almost 100 feet high. Such a wave can destroy buildings, uproot trees, and carry **debris** for miles.

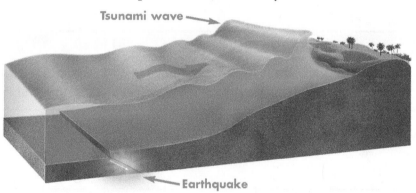

Tsunami wave

Earthquake

---

1. What can you infer about the danger faced by a ship far out at sea, where a tsunami first forms?

3. During a tsunami, why would it be safer to be on higher ground?

2. Why do you think a tsunami might be harmful to deep ocean life?

Practice reading with accuracy. Read every word and do not skip or substitute words.

FLUENCY

READ on your OWN
Nature in the Extreme, pages 29–31

VOCABULARY
Watch for the words you are learning about.

moderate: mild

rely: depend on

refreshed: replenished

FLUENCY
Be sure to read every word and do not substitute words.

BEFORE YOU READ

Think about the last pages you read in "Volcanic Eruptions." Why are mudflows dangerous?

AS YOU READ

Read "Steaming Up Again," pages 29–30.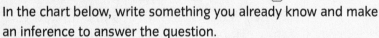
In the chart below, write something you already know and make an inference to answer the question.

Read "The Value of Volcanoes," page 31.
Write something you know and your inference in the chart.

Steaming Up Again	The Value of Volcanoes
Question Why do scientists use technology to monitor volcanoes?	**Question** How might volcanoes help produce life on Mars?
What I know	**What I know**
My inference	**My inference**

AFTER YOU READ

Do you think the advantages of volcanic eruptions outweigh the disadvantages? Why or why not?

Make Words Yours!

Learn the WORDS

Here are some words you will be reading in the next weeks. They are also words you need to know for your everyday reading.

WORD AND EXPLANATION	EXAMPLE	WRITE AN EXAMPLE
When you are **amid** something, you are surrounded by it, or in the middle of it.	We saw a few flowers **amid** the rocks.	When might you find yourself **amid** friends and family?
A **circuit** is the path of an electric current.	Tomás turned off the **circuit** before touching the wires.	What happens when you turn off a **circuit**?
When you **inquire** about something, you ask about it.	Did you **inquire** about the starting time of the game?	What have you **inquired** about so far today?
An **interval** is a space between things or a time between events.	There was a short **interval** between the lightning strike and the thunder.	What is another example of an **interval**?
Something that is a **plight** is an unfortunate or difficult situation.	The newspaper described the **plight** of the earthquake victims.	What is a **plight** you have heard about recently?
Somber describes something that is serious or gloomy.	His face was **somber** as he shared the bad news.	When might you wear **somber** clothes?
If things **topple**, they fall over or fall down.	Be careful you don't **topple** the pile of books!	What else can **topple**?
To **withstand** is to stand up to or to resist successfully.	The house was sturdy enough to **withstand** an earthquake.	Why is it hard to **withstand** criticism?

➤ YOUR TURN

Yes or No?

Answer these questions and be ready to explain your answers.

1. Is a birthday party usually a *somber* event? _____

2. Would you *inquire* about the weather before going to the beach? _____

3. Could finding money be a serious *plight*? _____

4. Can an electrical *circuit* be dangerous? _____

5. Is a minute a long *interval*? _____

6. Should you stand *amid* a herd of buffalo? _____

7. Could an ice storm *topple* a tree? _____

Now that you know the words, show what you know about earthquakes.

Choose the right word

| amid | circuit | inquire | interval |
| plight | somber | withstand | |

Fill each blank with the correct word from the box.

8. We stopped to _____ about the direction of the storm.

9. After the storm, a _____ announcer described the grim scene.

10. After a long _____ of silence, people began to speak.

11. We walked carefully _____ the damaged buildings.

12. The flagpole couldn't _____ the high winds.

13. The _____ of the storm survivors was serious.

14. The lamp won't work because Marcus turned off the _____ .

Show that you know

Complete the sentences.

15. Earthquakes can *topple* _____

16. To *withstand* an earthquake, a building should _____

READ on your OWN
Nature in the Extreme, pages 32–35

BEFORE YOU READ

Think about what you already know about earthquakes. What are some of the effects an earthquake can have when it strikes a city?

AS YOU READ

Read "Disaster!" pages 32–34.
In the chart below, write something you already know and make an inference to answer the question.

Read page 35 of "The Quake Hits."
Write something you know and your inference in the chart.

VOCABULARY
Watch for the words you are learning about.

topple: fall over

somber: serious

withstand: resist

FLUENCY
Be sure to read every word and do not skip or substitute words.

Disaster!	*The Quake Hits*
Question Why would the San Francisco earthquake have been less serious if it had happened in 1806 instead of 1906?	**Question** If you live near a fault line, what can you expect?
What I know	**What I know**
My inference	**My inference**

AFTER YOU READ

What do you think it would be like to experience an earthquake? Would you want to have the experience? Why or why not?

INFER: People in Nonfiction

How to Infer

Use **what you know**. Combine your experience with what you learned and what you read.	Use information about people, places, and events in **fiction** and **nonfiction**.	Use information to **predict** what will happen next in the text.	Identify the **causes**, or what made something happen, and the **effects**, or what happened.	Distinguish between those statements that are **facts** and those statements that are **opinions**.

Learn the STRATEGY

In nonfiction, the people you read about aren't made-up characters. They're real people. When you read a description of a person's experience in a nonfiction book, you know that the person really existed. You know that the experience really happened.

However, as you did with fiction, you can still make inferences. You use facts in the text, clues the writer gives you, and your personal experience and knowledge to guess how the person in the text was feeling or what he or she was thinking. Making inferences about people in nonfiction text can help you understand the information the text provides.

In the early 1900s, Enrico Caruso was one of the world's most famous opera singers. On April 18, 1906, however, Caruso was just one of the millions who experienced the San Francisco earthquake firsthand.

After performing in a concert in the city the night before, Caruso had gone to bed happy and pleased. He woke up a bit after 5:00 a.m. to find that his bed was shaking. Crossing to the window, he looked out and saw buildings falling over. As his hotel room rocked back and forth, he heard the sounds of screams outside. Caruso was convinced he must be dreaming.

Caruso left the hotel and boarded a train for New York City. Still, he could not relax. With each lurch of the train, Caruso was reminded of the rocking he had felt earlier. He would not soon forget his experience.

What can you infer about Caruso's concert the night before the earthquake?

a. The concert went well.

b. The concert took place on April 18, 1906.

c. Caruso performed with other famous singers.

During the earthquake, why did Caruso think he was dreaming?

a. He was seeing and hearing things that usually happen in nightmares.

b. He was rarely up that early.

c. He had a similar dream when he was younger.

YOUR TURN

Read "The Father of Seismology." Then answer the numbered questions.

THE FATHER OF SEISMOLOGY

Many people call John Milne the father of modern seismology, or earthquake research. Milne was born in Liverpool, England, in 1850. As a boy, he was serious and **somber** and liked to study earthquakes. He wanted to learn what caused the ground to shake so violently that it **toppled** buildings.

When Milne was 25, he accepted a job teaching in Tokyo, Japan. Milne was an adventurous man, but he suffered from the **plight** of seasickness. Getting to Japan from England would not be easy! Milne traveled by land all the way across Europe and Asia— thousands of miles out of his way!

Three months after leaving England, Milne finally reached Japan. He wasted no time getting back into his study of earthquakes. He founded the first seismological society in the world. He also invented tools that could be used to detect different types of earthquakes, measure the **intervals** between earthquake waves, and estimate the speeds at which earthquakes traveled.

An early seismograph, or tool for detecting earthquakes

Milne stayed in the country for 20 years, apparently settled for life. Then, in 1895, a fire destroyed his home and library. Milne quit his job and returned to England. The British government gave him money to set up a new laboratory to observe earthquakes. For the next 20 years, until Milne's death in 1913, his laboratory was the world headquarters for seismology.

1. What can you infer about why John Milne became a seismologist?

2. How did Milne feel about ocean travel?

What information in the text helped you make that inference?

3. Why do you think Milne returned to England in 1895?

4. Why do people call John Milne the father of seismology?

Change the expression in your voice to reflect whether information is surprising, serious, or descriptive.

FLUENCY

READ on your OWN
Nature in the Extreme, pages 36–38

BEFORE YOU READ

Think about the last pages you read in "San Francisco Shaking!" What caused most of the damage in the days that followed the 1906 earthquake?

AS YOU READ

Read "The First Shock," pages 36–37.
In the chart below, write something you already know and make an inference to answer the question.

Read "No Escape," page 38. (STOP)
Write something you know and your inference in the chart.

The First Shock	No Escape
Question Why didn't people in San Francisco have any warning that the earthquake was coming?	**Question** Why was the city not safe even after the earthquake?
What I know	**What I know**
My inference	**My inference**

AFTER YOU READ

Do you agree that animals can sense things that humans cannot? Explain your answer.

VOCABULARY
Watch for the words you are learning about.

toppled: fell down

amid: in the middle of

plight: dangerous situation

withstand: survive

FLUENCY
Change your expression and volume to match what you are reading.

Get Wordwise!
Identifying Synonyms and Antonyms

Learn More About the WORDS

Synonyms are words that have almost the same meanings.
High and *tall* are synonyms.

Antonyms are words with opposite meanings.
Short and *tall* are antonyms.

Complete the chart by circling synonyms and antonyms for the listed words.

WORD	CHOOSE THE SYNONYM	CHOOSE THE ANTONYM
You have to **enlarge** the hole to make the button fit.	expand, lessen, sew	swell, shrink, speed
The men should **heed** the advice of the police officer.	ignore, obey, speak	ignore, hear, lead
There was a lot of **debris** after the earthquake.	jewelry, trash, food	garbage, valuables, smog
We need to **inquire** about how to get there.	respond, ask, require	question, alert, answer
We watched the building **topple** to the ground.	fall, lift, throw	rise, trip, explode
Ted made sure the ladder was **secure** before climbing it.	slanted, safe, light	dangerous, upright, heavy
I was worried when I saw his **somber** face.	cheerful, angry, serious	serious, cheerful, upset

YOUR TURN

Choose the synonym

Write the word from the box that is a *synonym* for the underlined word.

1. We will <u>ask</u> if we can leave early. _____

2. The man's <u>serious</u> voice made everyone pay attention. _____

3. Everyone should <u>obey</u> the directions. _____

4. If the block tower is too tall, it will <u>fall</u>. _____

5. They swept the <u>trash</u> on the streets into big piles. _____

6. The homeowners wanted to <u>expand</u> their house. _____

> Show that you know the words by answering questions about natural disasters.

Choose the antonym

The sentences below don't make sense. Replace the underlined word with an *antonym* from the word box to the left so the sentence makes sense.

7. The earthquake caused the old tower to <u>rise</u>. _____

8. If you have a question, you should <u>answer</u> at the information booth. _____

9. The town is going to <u>shrink</u> the size of the park so that more kids can play in it. _____

10. The explosion scattered <u>valuables</u> everywhere. _____

11. Tony's mom wanted to move to a more <u>dangerous</u> neighborhood. _____

12. People should <u>ignore</u> the hurricane warnings and board up their houses. _____

Show that you know

Answer the questions. Use sentences.

13. During a natural disaster, what things might *topple*? _____

14. During a natural disaster, what things might *rise*? _____

READ on your OWN
Nature in the Extreme, pages 39–41

BEFORE YOU READ

Think about the last pages you read in "San Francisco Shaking!" What were some dangers faced by people who survived the 1906 San Francisco earthquake?

AS YOU READ

Read page 39 of "City on Fire!"
In the chart below, write something you already know and make an inference to answer the question.

Read "Doomed Buildings," pages 40–41.
Write something you know and your inference in the chart.

City on Fire!
Question Why did the fire travel so rapidly from one neighborhood to another?
What I know
My inference

Doomed Buildings
Question Why did the owner refuse to rent his building to Peter Bacigalupi for $500?
What I know
My inference

AFTER YOU READ

If you had been the store owner, would you have accepted Peter Bacigalupi's offer? Why or why not?

INFER: Use Inferences to Predict

How to Infer

Use **what you know**. Combine your experience with what you learned and what you read.	Use information about people, places, and events in **fiction** and **nonfiction**.	Use information to **predict** what will happen next in the text.	Identify the **causes**, or what made something happen, and the **effects**, or what happened.	Distinguish between those statements that are **facts** and those statements that are **opinions**.

Learn the STRATEGY

You've learned that when you infer, you put together what you already know with new information you are reading. One type of inference you can make is a prediction about what will happen next.

When you predict, you use what you read in the text and then make a guess about what will happen next using your experiences and knowledge. As you read further, you will discover whether your predictions were correct. Good readers are constantly making predictions and checking them as they read. Predictions will help you remember what you read. They will also make your reading more interesting.

Read the first paragraph. Then follow the directions in the side column.

Caroline had moved to California with her family 6 months before and so far had not felt an earthquake. Then one day at school she felt her desk shake. Suddenly, Mr. Lopez shouted, "Everyone under your desks!" Caroline was experiencing her first earthquake!

All the students quickly crouched under their desks. They had practiced this routine often in drills, so they knew what to do. The entire room was shaking. Caroline closed her eyes and tried to concentrate on staying calm. Then, as quickly as it had started, the shaking stopped, and she slowly opened her eyes and looked around at the mess surrounding her.

What predictions can you make about what will happen next in Caroline's classroom after reading the first paragraph?

_____

_____

_____

_____

Read the second paragraph. Which of your predictions actually happened?

_____

_____

_____

_____

What can you predict might happen next?

_____

_____

_____

_____

YOUR TURN

Read "A Letter to Abuela."
(*Abuela* means "grandmother.")
Then follow the numbered
directions.

A Letter to Abuela

1. Read the first paragraph.
Make a prediction about what
Benito will write about next.

2. Read the second paragraph.
What do you think will happen
next?

3. Read the third paragraph.
Did your predictions actually
happen?

Dear Abuela,

The earthquake this week was
unbelievable! I never realized how much
damage could be caused. The elevated
highway that my dad takes to his office
couldn't **withstand** the earthquake, and
portions of it **toppled** onto another
road. So, Dad hasn't been going to
work. Instead, we've started the tiring job of cleaning up.

At least I finally understand why Dad was always so
somber when he made us practice earthquake drills. I used
to think he was a little nutty about the subject, but when the
entire house started shaking, I was definitely glad I knew
what I was supposed to do.

Dad had told me that it was dangerous to be near
windows or the fireplace. I did what I had been told, and sure
enough, the picture window in the living room shattered into
a million pieces. I was safe under a doorway. Luckily Dad had
secured the heavy bookshelves to the living room wall with
huge bolts. Every single book tumbled off, but the
bookshelves stayed where they belonged. However, our
damage could have been worse. Many people suffered a
worse **plight**! Hopefully, by the time you visit, things will be
almost back to normal.

Love, Benito

4. Describe the types of experiences or knowledge you used to make
inferences about Benito's letter.

Imagine that you are Benito
talking to your grandmother.
Read the words in the letter
as if you were
having a
conversation.

FLUENCY

READ on your OWN
Nature in the Extreme, pages 42–44

BEFORE YOU READ

Think about the last pages you read in "San Francisco Shaking!" How might things have been different if most of San Francisco's homes and buildings had been made of brick instead of wood?

AS YOU READ

Read page 42 of "Fighting the Flames."
In the chart below, make a prediction about what will happen next.

Read "Fighting the Flames," pages 43–44.
Write whether your prediction was accurate and, if not, explain how the text was different.

Read the heading "Saving the Money!" page 44.
Make a prediction about what this section will be about. Then read the section and write whether your prediction was accurate. If not, explain how the text was different.

Fighting the Flames	*Saving the Money!*
My prediction	My prediction
Was it accurate? If not, how was the text different?	Was it accurate? If not, how was the text different?

AFTER YOU READ

How would you react if your home or workplace were blown up as a firebreak to protect other property?

INFER: Cause and Effect

How to Infer

Use **what you know**. Combine your experience with what you learned and what you read.

Use information about people, places, and events in **fiction** and **nonfiction**.

Use information to **predict** what will happen next in the text.

Identify the **causes**, or what made something happen, and the **effects**, or what happened.

Distinguish between those statements that are **facts** and those statements that are **opinions**.

Learn the STRATEGY

You have learned that to make inferences you put together information that you know with new information that you are reading about. You can also make inferences about causes and effects. An inference can be made about why something happened, the **cause**, as well as about what happened, the **effect**.

Suppose you notice that a tree outside your school has fallen after a storm. The effect is that the tree has fallen over. Think about what you know about strong storms. What inference can you make about why the tree was down—the cause? You may infer that the tree was blown over by a strong gust of wind. You are inferring this cause based on your knowledge of trees and storms.

Read the passage and then answer the questions in the side column.

Early in the morning on December 16, 1811, the people of New Madrid, Missouri, were jolted out of bed. They experienced the first in a series of violent earthquakes to hit the area that winter. These quakes were so powerful that they were felt all across the United States.

Few people lived in that part of the United States, so not many people died. The earthquakes' biggest impact was on the environment. About 150,000 acres of land were affected. New lakes were formed, cracks opened in the earth, trees were uprooted, and islands disappeared in the Mississippi River. The earthquakes even changed the course of the Mississippi River.

What **caused** the people of New Madrid, Missouri, to wake up on December 16, 1811?

a. They received an electric shock.
b. An earthquake struck their town.
c. They had to go to work or school.

Circle the **effects** of the earthquakes.

a. People died.
b. Lakes were formed.
c. Houses collapsed.
d. Cracks opened in the earth.
e. There were thunderstorms.
f. Trees were uprooted.

→ **YOUR TURN**

Read "Scheduling Earthquakes?" Then answer the numbered questions.

SCIENCE CONNECTION

Scheduling Earthquakes?

Secrets to Predicting In the mid-1970s, many scientists thought the secret to predicting earthquakes had been found. Chinese researchers had seemed to predict a major earthquake by studying the **intervals** between mild tremors. Their early warning had saved thousand of lives. Faith in this new method of prediction ended, however, when a huge earthquake unexpectedly struck northern China in 1976. **Amid** the confusion, more than 200,000 people were killed. Scientists had to start over. What, they **inquired**, was the secret to earthquake prediction?

The Law of Averages In the 1980s, U.S. scientists thought they had discovered a pattern. They realized that

If earthquakes could be predicted, many lives could be saved.

quakes strong enough to **topple** buildings had occurred near Parkfield, California, about every 22 years. They announced that a new quake would occur in 1988. The quake never happened. Scientists began to lose hope of ever finding a usable prediction tool.

The Work Continues Today, laser stations record the slightest movement along fault lines. Scientists have created risk maps that show where quakes might occur. Some researchers, though, believe the secret to predicting earthquakes lies in animal behavior; others focus on naturally occurring underground electrical currents. One day, a working earthquake prediction model might be found.

1. What was the effect of the Chinese researchers' prediction?

2. What was the effect of the 1976 earthquake in China?

3. What was an effect of the Parkfield earthquake prediction?

Look up unfamiliar words in a dictionary. When you reread, you'll understand the text better.

FLUENCY

READ on your OWN
Nature in the Extreme, pages 45–48

VOCABULARY
Watch for the words you are learning about.

toppling: falling down

somber: serious, sad

amid: in the middle of

FLUENCY
Look up the meanings of unfamiliar words as you read.

BEFORE YOU READ

Think about the last pages you read in "San Francisco Shaking!" How did having a new water system save the mint?

AS YOU READ

Read page 45 of "Amazing Escapes and Rescues." (STOP)
Fill in an effect for the cause stated in that part of the chart below.

Read page 46. (STOP)
Fill in a cause for the effect stated in that part of the chart.

Read page 47 of "Decision: Move or Stay?" (STOP)
Fill in a cause for the effect stated in that part of the chart.

Read page 48. (STOP)
Fill in a cause and an effect for that part of the chart.

Page	Cause	Effect
45	There were fires in the city of San Francisco.	
46		Some people tried to escape by moving to higher ground.
47		People used bicycles, baby strollers, wheelbarrows, pillowcases, or hired wagons.
48		

AFTER YOU READ

If you had to leave your home on foot, what is one thing you would take with you?

Make Words Yours!

Learn the WORDS

Here are some words you will be reading this week. They are also words you need to know for your everyday conversations.

WORD AND EXPLANATION	EXAMPLE	WRITE AN EXAMPLE
A **code** is a set of rules. A **code** can also be a system of words or symbols used to keep a message secret.	The local building **code** says every house must have a smoke detector.	What else might a building **code** require?
Something that is **elevated** is raised above the ground or another surface.	An **elevated** highway goes over part of downtown.	Why do bands perform on an **elevated** stage?
Fatigue means extreme tiredness or weariness.	Working long hours can cause **fatigue**.	When do you experience **fatigue**?
Something is **federal** if it is managed or required by the national government.	That judge works in the **federal** courthouse.	Would you like to have a **federal** job? Explain.
When you **restore** something, you bring it back to its original condition.	They plan to **restore** the old house.	What else could someone **restore**?
Something that is **tiring** causes fatigue or weariness.	A long hike can be **tiring**.	What else can be **tiring**?
Turmoil is great confusion.	After the earthquake, the city was in **turmoil**.	What other situations might cause **turmoil**?
A **version** is an account of an event or one side of things.	I heard a different **version** of the story from his.	When have you told your own **version** of a story?

YOUR TURN

Which word?

Circle the best answer to each question.

1. Which would be more *tiring*?
   a marathon or **a stroll**

2. Which one is *elevated*?
   a bridge or **a tunnel**

3. Which is a *code* of conduct in a library?
   silence or **sleeping**

4. Which is more likely to cause *fatigue*?
   running or **resting**

5. Which can be another *version* of a story?
   a play or **the alphabet**

6. Which would cause more *turmoil*?
   a traffic jam or **a picnic**

7. Which is a *federal* building?
   the White House or **a town library**

Now, show that you know the words by writing about earthquakes.

Choose the right word

federal	fatigue	restore	turmoil
elevated	code	tiring	version

Fill each blank with the correct word from the box.

8. There was so much [   ] that it was hard to know what was going on.

9. An [   ] train track was built above the street.

10. It will take months to [   ] the building to its original appearance.

11. It was [   ] to work all day without a break.

12. Which [   ] of the story do you believe?

13. The postal [   ] requires stamps on every envelope.

14. By the end of the day, a feeling of [   ] came over me.

15. Stealing someone else's mail can be a [   ] crime.

Show that you know

Use each word below in a sentence.

16. *turmoil*

17. *restore*

READ on your OWN
Nature in the Extreme, pages 49–51

BEFORE YOU READ

Think about the last pages you read in "San Francisco Shaking!" Why did people who stayed in the city try to get to higher ground?

AS YOU READ

Read page 49 of "Life and Death."
Fill in a cause and an effect in that part of the chart below.

Read "Life and Death," page 50.
Fill in a cause and an effect in that part of the chart.

Read "Coming to the Rescue," page 51.
Fill in a cause and an effect in that part of the chart.

VOCABULARY
Watch for the words you are learning about.

elevated: raised

turmoil: excitement and confusion

tiring: exhausting

FLUENCY
Reread texts with difficult words after you have looked up their definitions.

Life and Death, page 49	Life and Death, page 50	Coming to the Rescue
Cause	Cause	Cause
Effect	Effect	Effect

AFTER YOU READ

Choose a page and write about something you would tell a friend.

INFER:
Is It Fact or Opinion?

How to Infer

Use **what you know**. Combine your experience with what you learned and what you read.

Use information about people, places, and events in **fiction** and **nonfiction**.

Use information to **predict** what will happen next in the text.

Identify the **causes**, or what made something happen, and the **effects**, or what happened.

Distinguish between those statements that are **facts** and those statements that are **opinions**.

Learn the STRATEGY

When you make inferences, you use what you know to understand more about what you are reading. You can also make inferences using **facts** and **opinions**. First, though, you need to figure out whether what you are reading are facts or whether they are opinions.

How can you tell if you are reading facts or opinions? Remember that if you can research something to check that it is accurate, it's a fact. Opinions are personal feelings or beliefs. They can't be proved true or false. Also, phrases such as *In my opinion* or *I believe* are signals that the writer is probably stating an opinion.

Read the passage below and then follow the directions in the side column.

New buildings are definitely the safest places to be during an earthquake. Modern building techniques have made them more "earthquake proof." This means they are not as likely to collapse during an earthquake. I believe you will be injured if you are in an older building when an earthquake occurs. The building might sway or even topple over. Earthquakes can also damage electrical lines, telephone lines, and water pipes. Explosions and fires are caused by broken electric and gas lines. Powerful earthquakes also destroy homes and buckle roads.

Underline the sentences that contain only **facts**.

Circle a phrase that indicates that a sentence is an **opinion**.

Choose the sentence that is an **opinion** because it cannot be proved true or false.

a. The building might sway or even topple over.

b. New buildings are definitely the safest places to be during an earthquake.

c. Powerful earthquakes also destroy homes and buckle roads.

Which of the following is an inference based on the **facts** in the passage?

a. Older buildings suffer a lot of damage during earthquakes.

b. Not many people are injured by fires during earthquakes.

c. It's safe to travel right after an earthquake.

YOUR TURN

Read "Building for Earthquakes." Then follow the numbered directions.

1. Is the statement, "There is no way to construct an entirely earthquake-proof building," a fact or an opinion? How do you know?

2. Is the statement, "When there is an earthquake, the instruments measure and record what happens," a fact or an opinion? How do you know?

3. Is the statement, "When a quake shakes the ground, the base moves without shaking the entire building," a fact or an opinion? How do you know?

4. What types of changes can you infer will be made to future structures based on the last paragraph?

BUILDING FOR Earthquakes

There is no way to construct an entirely earthquake-proof building. However, scientists are learning how buildings can be made to better withstand the **turmoil** of an earthquake.

Studying the Effects of Earthquakes

In areas where earthquakes are frequent, scientific instruments are placed inside some buildings. When there is an earthquake, the instruments measure and record what happens. Scientists study this information to learn how earthquakes affect the buildings.

What Scientists Have Learned

One thing that scientists have learned is that some buildings are more likely to collapse than others. For example, buildings such as **elevated** parking garages have few inside walls. This kind of building is less secure than one with many inside walls. Scientists have also suggested changes to the building **code**. One change involves a system of springs or rollers placed at intervals in the base of a building. When a quake shakes the ground, the base moves without shaking the entire building.

Constructing buildings that resist earthquakes costs a lot. However, it is worth the money. It would be impossible to pass **federal** laws requiring buildings to be built this way. In areas where the threat of earthquakes is high, though, safe buildings are essential.

As you read, change your tone of voice to match the ideas you are reading about.

FLUENCY

READ on your OWN
Nature in the Extreme, pages 52–54

BEFORE YOU READ

Think about the last pages you read in "San Francisco Shaking!" Why did rescuers try to move artwork to the Fairmont Hotel?

AS YOU READ

Read pages 52–53 of "Relief Arrives."
Look at the sentence in that part of the chart below and decide whether it is a fact or an opinion. Then explain how you know. Finally, use it to make an inference.

Read "The Days After the Quake," page 54.
Follow the directions above.

VOCABULARY
Watch for the words you are learning about.

restored: brought back to original condition

codes: rules

fatigue: weariness

federal: belonging to the U.S. government

tiring: exhausting

FLUENCY
Read as if you were telling a story to someone.

Relief Arrives	*The Days After the Quake*
Fact or opinion? _____ You couldn't have done much except try to find a safe place to wait for help to arrive.	Fact or opinion? _____ On the day of the quake more than 30 babies were born in Golden State Park.
How do you know?	How do you know?
My inference	My inference

AFTER YOU READ

Would you like to live in San Francisco today? Why or why not?

Get Wordwise!
Understanding Analogies

Learn More About the WORDS

An **analogy** is made up of two pairs of words. The first two words go together in some way. The second two words go together in the same way.

This sentence is an synonym analogy:

Enlarge is to *increase* as *portion* is to *part*.

Enlarge and *increase* are synonyms. *Portion* and *part* are also synonyms.

The word pairs in an analogy can also show the relationship of a part to a whole.

Toe is to *foot* as *finger* is to *hand*.

Toe and *foot* go together for the same reason that *finger* and *hand* go together. The first word is a part and the second word is a whole.

COMPLETE THE ANALOGY	SYNONYMS OR PART TO WHOLE?
Classroom is to **school** as **chapter** is to _____. Which word best completes the analogy? ☐ train ☐ museum ☐ book	**Classroom** and **school** are _____.
Contented is to **satisfied** as **exhausting** is to _____. Which word best completes the analogy? ☐ restful ☐ tiring ☐ relaxing	**Contented** and **satisfied** are _____.
House is to **neighborhood** as **book** is to _____. Which word best completes the analogy? ☐ library ☐ house ☐ pencil	**House** and **neighborhood** are _____.
Topple is to **fall** as **scream** is to _____. Which word best completes the analogy? ☐ whisper ☐ motion ☐ yell	**Topple** and **fall** are _____.

YOUR TURN

Answer each question and be ready to explain your answers.

1. *Dwelling* is to *residence* as *area* is to *vicinity.* Synonym analogy? _____

2. *Petal* is to *flower* as *word* is to *dictionary.* Part to whole analogy? _____

3. *Debris* is to *treasure* as *ground* is to *sky.* Part to whole analogy? _____

4. *Secure* is to *dangerous* as *calm* is to *upset.* Synonym analogy? _____

Choose the right word

> neighborhood   turmoil
> circuit   code

Choose a word from the box to complete the analogy. Then tell if the first pair of words are synonyms or part to whole.

5. *Children* is to *family* as *dwelling* is to

   _____.

   Children and *family* are **part to whole /
   synonyms**.

6. *Person* is to *human* as *rule* is to

   _____.

   Person and *human* are **part to whole /
   synonyms**.

7. *Part* is to *piece* as *uproar* is to

   _____.

   Part and *piece* are **part to whole / synonyms**.

8. *Tongue* is to *mouth* as *current* is to

   _____.

   Tongue and *mouth* are **part to whole /
   synonyms**.

> Think about what you have read in this unit. Then write about the effects of earthquakes.

Show that you know

Answer the questions. Use sentences.

9. Why might people feel *fatigue* after an earthquake?

   _____

   _____

10. What kind of buildings do you think should be *restored* first after an earthquake? Why?

    _____

    _____

    _____

11. What might an *elevated* structure look like after an earthquake?

    _____

    _____

12. What kind of *turmoil* could there be after an earthquake?

    _____

    _____

READ on your OWN
Nature in the Extreme, **pages 55–57**

BEFORE YOU READ

Think about the last pages you read in "San Francisco Shaking!" What do you think the people of San Francisco will do to rebuild their city?

AS YOU READ

Read page 55 of "Back to the Future."
Look at the sentence in that part of the chart below and decide whether it is a fact or an opinion. Then explain how you know. Finally, use it to make an inference.

Read "San Francisco Lives Again!" pages 56–57.
Follow the directions above.

Back to the Future	*San Francisco Lives Again!*
Fact or opinion? _____ "The work of rebuliding San Franscisco has commenced, and I expect to see the great metropolis replaced on a much grander scale than ever before."	**Fact or opinion?**_____ One Oregon school for Native Americans baked 830 loaves of bread for hungry city residents.
How do you know?	**How do you know?**
My inference	**My inference**

AFTER YOU READ

What lesson do you think we can learn from the way the city of San Francisco responded to the disaster?

VOCABULARY
Watch for the words you are learning about.

fatigued: tired

restore: bring back to original condition

restoration: act of repairing something

federal: belonging to the U.S. government

version: form that varies from the original

FLUENCY
Read as if you are having a conversation with someone.

INFER: Put It All Together

How to Infer

Use **what you know**. Combine your experience with what you learned and what you read.

Use information about people, places, and events in **fiction** and **nonfiction**.

Use information to **predict** what will happen next in the text.

Identify the **causes**, or what made something happen, and the **effects**, or what happened.

Distinguish between those statements that are **facts** and those statements that are **opinions**.

Learn the STRATEGY

Making inferences means using what you know to figure out a meaning not stated in the text you are reading. It helps you understand and remember what you read. It makes your reading more interesting and personal. To make an inference, you put together what you know with what you read.

Your personal experiences are part of what you know. You can use your personal experiences to help you make inferences and go beyond the text. What you've learned—in school, and at home, and from friends—is also part of what you know. You can use inferences to do the following:

• to better understand the places and characters in **fiction** and the people and concepts in textbooks and other **nonfiction**.
• to **predict**, or make a guess about what will happen next.
• to recognize **causes** or **effects**.
• to tell **fact** from **opinion**.

In large earthquakes, entire buildings and bridges may break apart. However, not all structures are destroyed. Some survive with little damage because of their design. Flexible moorings are used routinely in most earthquake zones today. The moorings are made of steel plates with rubber and steel disks. They are attached to the base of the structure and the ground. During an earthquake, the moorings move with the seismic waves. The rubber disks absorb most of the vibrations, letting the building gently sway rather than crumble.

Based on what you read in this passage and what you already know about earthquakes, what inference can be made about building structures in earthquake zones?

a. Flexible moorings help keep structures stable.
b. Flexible moorings are used everywhere today in new building construction.
c. Seismic waves move moorings back and forth.

What did you already know about earthquakes that helped you make this inference?

_____

_____

_____

Did you make any other inferences while reading this passage? What were they?

_____

_____

_____

_____

▶ YOUR TURN

Read "Bridge Rebuilding."
Then answer the numbered
questions.

BRIDGE REBUILDING
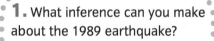

Since it opened in 1937, the Golden Gate Bridge has been a symbol of San Francisco. However, after the 1989 earthquake, people were worried. They feared that the bridge would not be able to withstand an even more powerful earthquake.

The bridge could be replaced with an identical one that met modern building **codes**. However, doing so would cost more than $2 billion! Still, no one wanted to save money by building a simpler **version** of the bridge. Officials decided to **restore** the bridge instead, at a cost of almost $400 million.

Increased tolls mean that everyone who uses the bridge is helping to pay for the work. Because the bridge is part of the National Highway System, **federal** funds can also be used.

Work started in 1997 and will continue for at least 10 years. When the project is completed, the people of San Francisco will still have their beautiful bridge. It will also be strong enough to handle an earthquake of up to magnitude 8.3.

1. What inference can you make about the 1989 earthquake?

What did you already know that helped you make this inference?

2. What inference can you make about modern building codes?

3. What are two other inferences you can make based on the last two paragraphs of the passage?

Read at a comfortable pace, as if you were talking to someone about the different ways of saving the bridge.

FLUENCY

READ on your OWN
Nature in the Extreme, pages 58–60

BEFORE YOU READ

Think about the last pages you read in "San Francisco Shaking!" How did city officials help business owners after the San Francisco earthquake in 1906?

VOCABULARY
Watch for the words you are learning about.

federal: belonging to the U.S. government

elevation: height of an area of land

codes: laws

FLUENCY
Read at a comfortable pace, as if you were talking to someone.

AS YOU READ

Read page 58 of "A Bright Future."
In the chart below, write something you already know and make an inference to answer the question.

Read page 59.
Write something you know and your inference in the chart.

Read page 60.
Write something you know and your inference in the chart.

Page 58	Page 59	Page 60
Question How could a major earthquake in modern San Francisco cause someone in another part of the country to lose his or her job?	**Question** If the USGS announces that a major quake is about to strike San Francisco, what could be done to protect people and property?	**Question** What could your family do to make your home safer during an earthquake?
What I know	**What I know**	**What I know**
My inference	**My inference**	**My inference**

AFTER YOU READ

What do you think is one important lesson officials learned by studying the 1906 earthquake?

Unit 6 Reflection

VOCABULARY

The easiest way for me to learn new words is

Some words I still need to work on are

Nature in the Extreme

COMPREHENSION

One thing I learned about making inferences is

Inferring helps me

I can improve my inferences by

FLUENCY

One thing that helps me read more smoothly is

The hardest thing about reading out loud is

INDEPENDENT READING

To me, the most interesting thing about Nature in the Extreme is

SUCCESS STORIES

unit 7

COMPREHENSION

LEARN TO UNDERSTAND HOW TO USE READING STRATEGIES—AND WHEN TO USE THEM

INDEPENDENT READING

Success Stories
Includes "Remarkable Kids" and "Right Under Your Nose"

VOCABULARY

WORDS:
Know them!
Use them!
Learn all about them!

FLUENCY

Make your reading smooth and accurate, one tip at a time.

Make Words Yours!

Learn the WORDS

Here are some words you will be reading in the next week. They are also words you need to know for your everyday reading.

WORD AND EXPLANATION	EXAMPLE	WRITE AN EXAMPLE
An **adventure** is an exciting experience that can sometimes be dangerous.	Our ride on the sailboat that windy day was an **adventure**.	What **adventures** might you plan for your next vacation?
Your **attitude** is the way you act, or behave, that shows how you are feeling.	Ryan's friendly **attitude** made me feel welcome.	Who do you know who has a positive **attitude**?
Characteristics are the things that make a person different from someone else.	Friendliness and kindness are two **characteristics** that made my uncle very special.	What **characteristics** do you look for in a friend?
If something is a **feat**, it is an act that shows great courage, skill, or strength.	Climbing to the top of the mountain was a remarkable **feat**.	What **feats** has your favorite athlete accomplished?
People or things that **flourish** do well, grow, or are successful.	The flowers they planted **flourished** in the rich soil and warm sunlight.	What type of business would **flourish** near your school?
If something has **intensity**, it has great concentration or strength.	Kate was studying with such **intensity** that she didn't hear the phone ring.	What are some other things that might have great **intensity**?
When you **pursue** something, you follow or chase it in order to catch or get it.	The police officer **pursued** the thief.	What career would you like to **pursue**?
Undoubtedly means certainly, surely, or without doubt.	The weather report says it will **undoubtedly** snow today.	Who do you think is **undoubtedly** the best music group?

YOUR TURN

Answer these questions and be ready to explain your answers.

1. Is going to the mall an *adventure*?

_____

2. If I say something *flourished*, does that mean that it did well? _____

3. If something is *undoubtedly* true, is it false?

_____

4. Is eating my breakfast a great *feat*?

_____

Choose the right word

> adventure   attitude   characteristics   feat
> flourish   intensity   undoubtedly   pursue

Fill each blank with the correct word.

5. I will _____ need to wear a winter coat today.

6. The _____ of honesty and kindness make Ray a good friend.

7. Luke's caring _____ will make him a great doctor.

8. Our mountain climbing _____ was something we would always remember.

9. Toby and Gina _____ in school and will get good jobs.

10. The _____ of the fog kept planes from leaving the airport.

11. I saw the cat _____ the mouse.

12. Climbing to the top of the rope in gym class was a great _____.

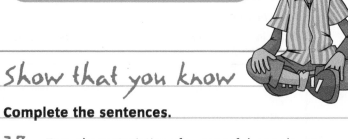

Show that you know the words by writing about successful people.

Show that you know

Complete the sentences.

13. Two *characteristics* of successful people are

_____

_____

14. In order to *pursue* their goals, successful people

_____

_____

15. Successful people work with *intensity*

because _____

_____

_____

16. It is important for successful people to have a positive *attitude* because

_____

_____

_____

READ on your OWN
Success Stories, pages 3–6

BEFORE YOU READ

Think about what you already know about the achievements of some young people. What do you think drives young people to make extraordinary achievements?

AS YOU READ

Read pages 3–5 of "Standing Up to Pressure."
Answer the questions.
What issues are Tyrel Bernardini concerned about?

_____

_____

What kind of volunteer work does Thais Baldini do?

_____

_____

Read page 6 of "A Brave Heart."
Answer the question.
What did Rudy Garcia-Tolson do at age 5 that was so amazing?

_____

_____

AFTER YOU READ

Choose a person in this section and tell what you would like to find out about him or her.

VOCABULARY
Watch for the words you are learning about.

flourish: to succeed or thrive

attitudes: a person's states of mind or opinions

undoubtedly: not disputed; certainly

feat: an act showing unusual daring, skill, or endurance

FLUENCY
Pay attention to punctuation. Pause briefly when you come to end marks.

METACOGNITION: Thinking About Thinking

What Good Readers Do

Before reading
- Preview.
- Think about the topic.
- Ask questions.
- Make predictions.

During reading
- Identify the topic, main idea, and details.
- Identify text structure, ask questions, visualize, make inferences.
- Reread.

After reading
- Summarize.
- Ask questions.
- Use graphic organizers to organize information.

Learn the STRATEGY

Good readers often think about how they are reading. They think about what they are doing that helps them understand what they read. They also think about some of the things they can do that will help them to better understand what they read.

You have learned many different strategies that help you to read better. These strategies are summarizing, questioning, predicting, text structure, visualizing, and inferring. Think about how you use each strategy. Here are some things that good readers do:

Miriam: "Before I read, I read the title and the headings to give me an idea of what I'm going to be reading about."

Julius: "As I read, I ask myself *Who? What? When? Where? Why?* and *How?* questions. Asking these types of questions helps me to better understand what I'm reading."

Kevin: "After I read, I state the main idea and important details in my words. I remember what I read better if I put things in my own words."

Before you read…

Think about what you do before you read. Then check the boxes that apply.

☐ Do you preview the text?
☐ Do you read the title and headings?
☐ Do you think about what you already know about the topic?
☐ Do you set a goal for reading?

How does thinking about what you are doing help you as you read?

_____

_____

_____

YOUNG MUSICAL GENIUS

One of the most gifted musicians of all time wrote his first musical composition before he was even seven years old. He toured Europe before he was ten. During that tour, he performed his own compositions on several different instruments. The crowds went wild! Wolfgang Amadeus Mozart lived from 1756 to 1791. He died at a young age, but he left the world with a treasure of intricate musical works.

YOUR TURN

Preview "Young Stars" and answer the first question. Then read the passage and answer the other questions.

YOUNG STARS

Have you ever watched a TV show or a movie with a baby as a main character? If so, you were probably watching two babies playing the part of that one character. Viewers don't notice because the twins switch places every so often.

The Big Break Babies aren't the easiest people to work with. There are laws that limit the number of hours that child actors can work. That's why producers try to find twins to share a part. However, it is no small **feat** to win the part of a baby, even if you are twins. Hundreds of sets of twins audition for the same part. To get the big break, it helps to be adorable, well behaved, and have good **attitudes**!

Growing Up on Screen The **intensity** of working as a child actor can cause many problems. Moviemakers try hard to make the set a good place to work. Dressing rooms are full of games. Child actors often get together to play with other kids their age. Some children get special schooling on the set. Other child actors are able to attend regular school.

Undoubtedly, keeping life as normal as possible helps child actors. Many child actors leave acting to live regular lives. Others continue to perform in TV shows and movies. Some even make music videos, have a line of toys, or star in a book series!

1. What did you do before you read the passage? Check the boxes that apply.
   - ☐ Did you preview the text?
   - ☐ Did you read the title?
   - ☐ Did you think about what you would like to learn?

2. How did your preview of the passage help you understand it?

3. What might you do differently before you read next time?

As you read and reread, pay attention to punctuation marks that are clues to correct phrasing.

FLUENCY

READ on your OWN
Success Stories, pages 7–9

BEFORE YOU READ

Think about the pages you read before. Why were Rudy Garcia-Tolson's legs amputated?

AS YOU READ

Preview pages 7–9 and answer the question.
What did you do before you read the pages?
Check the boxes that apply.

☐ Did you preview the text?

☐ Did you read the title?

☐ Did you look at the picture?

☐ Did you think about what you already know about the topic?

☐ Did you think about what you would like to learn?

☐ Did you set a goal for reading?

Read pages 7–9.
Answer the questions.
How did your preview of the pages help you understand them?

_____

_____

What might you do differently before you read next time?

_____

_____

VOCABULARY
Watch for the words you are learning about.

flourished: succeeded or thrived

intense: greatly concentrated

feat: an act showing unusual daring, skill, or endurance

undoubtedly: not disputed; certainly

pursue: to follow a path toward something

attitude: a person's state of mind or opinion

intensity: with extra energy or activity

FLUENCY
Let your voice rise slightly at the end of a question.

AFTER YOU READ

Choose a page and tell about something on that page that surprised you.

Get Wordwise!
Using Context Clues

Learn More About the WORDS

As you know, words and phrases that help you figure out the
meaning of an unfamiliar word are called **context clues**. There are
many different kinds of context clues. Sometimes there is a familiar
word next to the word you do not know. At times, the sentence
may include a definition of the word or a synonym. Other times, an
example will be given. All of these context clues will help you
know what a new word means.

EXAMPLE SENTENCE	USE CONTEXT CLUES
The **characteristics** that helped her succeed are a positive attitude and a willingness to help others.	What clues tell you that **characteristics** are qualities and features that make a person different?
Rudy's success at the Paralympics was an amazing **feat** for someone so young.	How do you know that a **feat** is an act that shows great courage, skill, or strength?
The children **flourished** and improved immensely with the attention of the individual volunteers.	What words tell you the meaning of **flourished**?
The camp was only a week long, but the **intensity**, or strength, of the program made up for the lack of time.	What definition is given for **intensity**?
The girls would not give up and **pursued** their goal until they reached it.	How do you know that **pursued** means followed or chased something?
Surely, **undoubtedly**, their hard work was critical to their success.	What word means the same as **undoubtedly**?

YOUR TURN

Use context clues and familiar word parts to decide the meaning of the underlined word. Then write *yes* or *no* to tell whether the word in the box is a synonym for it.

FIND CONTEXT CLUES	SYNONYM?	YES/NO?
1. The <u>intensity</u> with which he worked helped him succeed.	concentration	
2. The band <u>flourished</u> with the help of the volunteer music teacher.	failed	
3. <u>Undoubtedly</u>, their attention to detail helped them win the prize.	surely	
4. Jack <u>pursued</u> his dream to become a teacher.	lost	

Circle the word

Circle the correct word in each pair.

5. The soccer team **pursued / flourished** their goal of a championship.

6. The goalie's amazing save was the **feat / characteristic** that won the game.

7. The team **pursued / flourished** under the coach's direction.

8. The **feat / characteristic** that set the team apart from others was the ability to work together.

9. Joe played with such **intensity / undoubtedly** that the other team was scared of him.

10. Stacey was **intensity / undoubtedly** the best guitar player in the band.

Show that you know

characteristics	feat	flourished
intensity	pursued	undoubtedly

> Show that you know the words by writing about someone you know who met a challenge and succeeded.

Write four sentences. In each, use one of the words from the box.

11.

12.

13.

14.

READ on your OWN
Success Stories, pages 10–12

VOCABULARY
Watch for the words you are learning about.

adventures: unusual or exciting experiences

characteristics: distinguishing features or styles

FLUENCY
Remember to let your voice drop when you come to a period and rise when you come to an exclamation mark.

BEFORE YOU READ

Think about what you read in the past few days. What did Rudy accomplish at the 2004 Paralympics?

AS YOU READ

Preview pages 10–12 and answer the question.
What did you do before you read the pages?
Check the boxes that apply.

☐ Did you preview the text?

☐ Did you read the title?

☐ Did you look at the picture?

☐ Did you think about what you already know about the topic?

☐ Did you think about what you would like to learn?

☐ Did you set a goal for reading?

Read pages 10–12 of "Eco Adventures."
Answer the questions.
How did your preview of the pages help you understand them?

_____

_____

What might you do differently before you read next time?

_____

_____

AFTER YOU READ

Why do you think it's important to help endangered or injured animals?

METACOGNITION: Thinking About Summarizing

What Good Readers Do

Before reading
- Preview.
- Think about the topic.
- Ask questions.
- Make predictions.

During reading
- Identify the topic, main idea, and details.
- Identify text structure, ask questions, visualize, make inferences.
- Reread.

After reading
- Summarize.
- Ask questions.
- Use graphic organizers to organize information.

Learn the STRATEGY

You know that summarizing helps you identify the most important ideas in a passage. Think about what you do before, during, and after you read in order to summarize. A good reader thinks about summarizing in the following way:

- Before I read, I know I need to identify the topic. So I ask myself, "What is this passage about, and what is the most important idea the writer has to say about it?"
- As I read, I circle the main idea. Then I underline any important details.
- After I read, I review the main idea and put it into my own words. Then I use the details I underlined and the main idea to summarize.

Think about how to summarize the following journal entry.

> March 30, 1869
>
> Lime Rock Lighthouse, Newport, RI
> Yesterday my brother and I made a difficult rescue. A snow squall came up as several men tried to row their way to Fort Adams. Mother saw them capsize in the frigid water and summoned me from bed. My brother and I jumped into the boat and rowed out to the overturned vessel. We were able to retrieve the two soldiers, but alas, the young man escorting them was lost.

What did you do before you read to prepare yourself to summarize?

_____

_____

_____

_____

What did you do during reading to prepare yourself to summarize the passage? Check the boxes that apply.

☐ Did you circle the main idea?
☐ Did you underline important details?
☐ Did you restate the main idea and details in your own words?

How were these steps useful in preparing yourself to summarize after you read?

_____

_____

_____

_____

_____

➤ YOUR TURN

Preview "Honoring Our Hometown Heroine." Then read the passage and think about how you would summarize it.

1. What did you do before you read to prepare yourself to summarize?

2. What did you do during reading to summarize the passage?

3. How were these steps useful in preparing yourself to summarize after you read?

JULY 5, 1869

Honoring Our Hometown Heroine

Newport Recognizes Ida Lewis

Sailing has **flourished** at Newport Harbor. Many thanks belong to the lighthouse keeper. At the Fourth of July celebration, the residents of Newport, Rhode Island, thanked Miss Ida Lewis of the Lime Rock Lighthouse. Miss Lewis was given a beautiful new boat named *Rescue*. The **characteristics** of this splendid vessel include red velvet cushions and gold-plated oarlocks. It is an expression of the community's gratitude for this young woman's lifesaving efforts. The ever-humble Miss Lewis acknowledged this gift by saying, "Thank you. Thank you—I don't deserve it."

A History of Helping

In a speech, the mayor spoke of Miss Lewis's **adventure** rescuing two soldiers. "Those fellows were lucky. Ida has been known as the best swimmer in these parts since she was 14," he said. "She's been a blessing to this community." Miss Lewis built her strength rowing her younger siblings to school so they could **pursue** their studies. She had tended the lighthouse and saved many people since she was 16 years old. One of her most memorable rescues took place in 1867. Miss Lewis not only saved three men in a sinking boat, she also went back to save their sheep!

Scan the passage for words you don't know.
Practice reading these words ahead of time.

READ on your OWN
Success Stories, **pages 13–15**

BEFORE YOU READ

Think about what you read over the past few days. What does the Roots & Shoots program do?

AS YOU READ

Read pages 13–15 of "A Determined Young Woman." Answer the questions.

What did you do before you read to prepare yourself to summarize?

_____

_____

What did you do during reading to help you prepare yourself to summarize the passage? Give an example of each step.

- I identified the topic. Example: _____

- I identified the main idea. Example: _____

_____

- I underlined important details. Examples: _____

_____

_____

- I restated the main idea and details. Example:

_____

_____

How were these steps useful in preparing yourself to summarize after you read?

_____

_____

AFTER YOU READ

What do you think is the most important reason for a person to learn to read?

VOCABULARY
Watch for the words you are learning about.

flourished: succeeded or thrived

pursued: followed a path toward something

adventure: an unusual or exciting experience

intensity: with extra energy or activity

FLUENCY
Use punctuation. Pause when you come to commas and periods.

Make Words Yours!

Learn the WORDS

As you read more about remarkable kids, you'll come across these words. Here is your chance to get to know them better.

WORD AND EXPLANATION	EXAMPLE	WRITE AN EXAMPLE
To **dedicate** is to give attention, time, and effort to something you think is important.	The basketball player was **dedicated** to helping her team win the championship.	Why might people **dedicate** their lives to helping other people?
When you give **funding** to a project or purpose, you give money to it.	The large companies in our town gave **funding** for scholarship programs.	What would you like to provide **funding** for in your community?
To **inspire** is to motivate or create a strong desire to do something good.	Great teachers often **inspire** their students to be the best that they can.	What **inspires** you?
If something is an **issue**, it is a subject or problem that people need to talk about.	Our town's leaders debated the **issue** of raising our taxes.	What important **issues** do you discuss with your friends?
Someone is **passionate** when he or she has or shows strong feelings or emotions, such as anger or love.	Tyrone's **passionate** desire to help people led him to become a doctor.	What do you feel **passionate** about?
Something that is **satisfying** gives a person pleasure and meets his or her needs or wishes.	It was **satisfying** to get a good grade after studying all week.	What would you consider a **satisfying** meal?
When a person does something **voluntarily**, it means he or she freely chooses to do it.	Jim **voluntarily** helped out by cleaning the entire house.	What actions might you do **voluntarily** to help around the classroom?
Something is **worthwhile** when it is worth your time, effort, or attention.	Megan and Nicole collected canned food for the homeless because it was a **worthwhile** cause.	Why is it **worthwhile** to learn to type?

YOUR TURN

True or False?

Decide whether each statement is true or false. Be ready to explain your answers.

1. When you are *dedicated*, it means you don't care. _____

2. If we give *funding* to a project, we give money to it. _____

3. If a meal is *satisfying*, it tastes bad. _____

4. When you *inspire* someone, you motivate that person to do something right. _____

Choose the right word

> funding   inspire   issue   worthwhile
> passionate satisfying voluntarily

Fill each blank with the correct word.

5. Pam showed strong emotions when she talked about birds. _____

6. We needed to discuss an important problem. _____

7. David chose to help us sweep the deck. _____

8. It is worth your time and effort to read this book. _____

9. The principal will give money for our special project. _____

10. Teachers motivate their students to do well. _____

11. The meal was perfect! _____

> What would you like to be successful in? Show that you know the words by finishing the sentences about your goal.

Show that you know

Complete the sentences.

12. A goal I am *dedicated* to and feel *passionate* about is

13. My goal is *worthwhile* because

14. To learn more about my goal I could *voluntarily*

15. Some *issues* I may face as I reach for my goal are

READ on your OWN
Success Stories, pages 16–19

BEFORE YOU READ

Think about the last pages you read. How was Thais able to overcome her learning disability?

AS YOU READ

Read pages 16–19 of "A Confident Voice."
Answer the questions.

What did you do before you read to prepare yourself to summarize?

_____

_____

What did you do during reading to prepare yourself to summarize the passage?

_____

_____

How were these steps useful in preparing yourself to summarize after you read?

_____

_____

AFTER YOU READ

Choose the most interesting section in pages 16–19. What is one new fact you learned?

METACOGNITION: Thinking About Questioning

What Good Readers Do

Before reading
- Preview.
- Think about the topic.
- Ask questions.
- Make predictions.

During reading
- Identify the topic, main idea, and details.
- Identify text structure, ask questions, visualize, make inferences.
- Reread.

After reading
- Summarize.
- Ask questions.
- Use graphic organizers to organize information.

Learn the STRATEGY

Think about the kinds of questions you ask before you read, as you read, and after you read. When you ask questions and think about the answers, you think more deeply about the text.

Different people ask different kinds of questions.
- Before he reads, Jeff asks, "What do I already know about this topic? How can I use what I know to better understand the text?"
- As he reads, Marco asks *Who? What? When? Where? Why?* and *How?* questions.
- After she reads, Julia asks, "What did I learn from this text?"

What kinds of questions do you ask before you read, as you read, and after you read? Now think about why you ask these kinds of questions.

Nine-year-old Christian Whitton was upset. One of his best friends had wanted to play in the local football league but had been turned away. The coaches felt that a physically challenged boy shouldn't play.

However, Christian felt that his friend should be able to play. Christian got information about the rights of disabled and physically challenged individuals. He used this information to persuade the league to let his friend play. Since then, Christian has continued to help physically challenged people.

Think about the questions you ask before, during, and after your read a passage. Check the boxes that apply.

☐ Before I read, I ask questions about the topic.

☐ I ask myself what I want to learn.

☐ As I read, I ask myself *Who? What? When? Where? Why?* and *How?* questions.

☐ I reread to find the answers to these questions.

☐ After I read, I ask myself if I learned what I had hoped to learn.

☐ I ask "How can I learn more about this topic?"

➤ YOUR TURN

Preview "Making a Difference." Think about the questions you have from your preview. Then read the passage and answer the questions.

1. Think about the questions you asked. Check the boxes that apply.

☐ Before you read, did you ask yourself what you already know about the topic?

☐ As you read, did you ask yourself *Who? What? When? Where? Why?* and *How?* questions?

☐ As you read, did you ask yourself *How are the people in the text like me?*

☐ After you read, did you ask yourself what you had hoped to learn?

2. Think about the questions you asked as you read. Why did you ask those questions?

Making a DIFFERENCE

Students assemble to rake the lawn of an elderly neighbor. Teenagers meet at a homeless shelter to entertain the children who live there. These **worthwhile** activities are examples of what Kids Care Clubs are all about.

Who are these people?

Kids Care Clubs started in 1990 in Connecticut. Debbie Spaide wanted to promote **voluntary** service. She organized a group of students to help people in the community. Under her direction, the program's popularity grew. The program eventually expanded to include young people from all 50 states and from other countries such as Australia, Canada, and Germany.

How does it work?

Individuals who participate in Kids Care Clubs do so for one simple reason—to help others. Each month, **dedicated** students select a service project. The projects address issues such as poverty, literacy, or homelessness. Working together, participants might prepare food, provide tutoring, or work at shelters.

What does it take to get started?

Kids Care Clubs are provided with an array of materials. Project suggestions and recommendations on **funding** activities are also included. If you would like to organize a Kids Care Club in your community, visit the Web site—www.kidscare.org, and see how you can make a difference, too!

Subheads provide natural breaks in the passage. Reread the selection. Pause before and after you read each subhead.

READ on your OWN
Success Stories, pages 20–22

BEFORE YOU READ

Think about what you read over the past few days. How did Keisha's family help her start her own clothing line?

AS YOU READ

Preview pages 20–22 of "A Community Leader."
Fill in the "Before reading" section of the chart below with any questions you have.

Then read pages 20–22.
Fill in the chart with questions you asked yourself during reading and after reading.

Reading stages	Questions	Why did you decide to ask these questions?
Before reading		
During reading		
After reading		

AFTER YOU READ

What unusual building materials do you think people could use to build houses? Why?

VOCABULARY
Watch for the words you are learning about.

worthwhile: of real value

funding: money set aside for a special purpose

voluntarily: willingly

FLUENCY
To help make your reading smoother, preview the text and make sure you know how to pronounce difficult words.

Get Wordwise!
Homophones and Homographs

Learn More About the WORDS

Homophones are words that are pronounced the same but have different meanings and are usually spelled differently. Here are some common homophones.

HOMOPHONE PAIRS	WRITE THE HOMOPHONE
feat: an act showing great courage, skill, or strength **feet:** the plural form of the word *foot*; your feet are part of your body.	Kyra put her _____ in the pool. Winning first prize was a great _____ for Mikal.
lessen: to reduce or make something less **lesson:** something to be taught or studied	The forecast said the rain will _____ tonight. I took a driving _____ before I got my license.
root: the underground part of a plant **route:** a road or course that someone travels	When digging in the garden, I hit a tree _____. Which _____ will you take to get to the store?

Homographs are words that are spelled the same but have different meanings. Sometimes the words are pronounced differently, too. You can discover the meaning by reading the whole sentence. Here are some common homographs.

HOMOGRAPH PAIRS	NOUN OR VERB?
issue **n.:** a problem that needs to be discussed **v.:** to give or supply something to someone	One **issue** we need to talk about is money. _____ The school will **issue** ten pencils to every student. _____
tire **n.:** a band of rubber around the edge of a wheel **v.:** to feel in need of rest or sleep	I **tire** quickly when I listen to slow music. _____ We changed the bike's flat **tire**. _____
fund **n.:** money set aside for a special reason **v.:** to put aside money for a special reason	The company will **fund** our team so we can buy uniforms. _____ The scholarship **fund** helped Jill pay for college. _____

YOUR TURN

Choose the homophone

Circle the correct homophone in each pair.

1. Swimming across the lake was a great **feat / feet**.

2. The weed's **root / route** grew throughout my garden.

3. I took a short **root / route** to school today.

4. Standing outside in the snow made our **feat / feet** very cold.

Choose the right word

feat/feet	lessen/lesson	root/route
issue	tire	fund

Fill each blank with the correct word from the box.

5. The teacher will _____ our homework if we are good.

6. The car's _____ was flat, so we pumped it up.

7. The clown was wearing huge shoes on his _____ .

8. We debated the _____ until midnight.

9. The ship's _____ was marked on the map.

10. They needed to _____ supplies to the soldiers.

11. The town will _____ a new statue.

Show that you know about homophones and homographs. Write about inventions.

Show that you know

Complete the sentences.

12. If an inventor *tires* of inventing, he or she should _____

13. A special *fund* can help an inventor because _____

14. One *lesson* people can learn from inventors is _____

READ on your OWN
Success Stories, pages 23–25

BEFORE YOU READ

Think about what you read in the past few days. Why did Lucretia and her friends build a house out of straw?

AS YOU READ

Preview pages 23–25 of "He's Got the Beat."
Fill in the "Before reading" section of the chart below with any questions you have.

Then read pages 23–25.
Fill in the chart with questions you had during reading and after reading.

Reading stages	Questions	Why did you decide to ask these questions?
Before reading		
During reading		
After reading		

VOCABULARY
Watch for the words you are learning about.

inspire: to encourage, impress, or serve as an example for

satisfaction: the condition of having a feeling of well-being

passionate: having or showing strong feelings about something

fund: to give money for a special purpose

FLUENCY
Rereading will help you to read more smoothly and remember the information.

AFTER YOU READ

Choose a section in pages 23–25. Decide what information in that section you would like to share with someone else.

METACOGNITION
Thinking About Predicting

What Good Readers Do

Before reading
- Preview.
- Think about the topic.
- Ask questions.
- Make predictions.

During reading
- Identify the topic, main idea, and details.
- Identify text structure, ask questions, visualize, make inferences.
- Reread.

After reading
- Summarize.
- Ask questions.
- Use graphic organizers to organize information.

Learn the STRATEGY

You know that previewing and predicting are good things to do before you read. They help you prepare to read. One class discussed how previewing and predicting help them understand what they read. Here are their ideas:

Melissa: "Previewing the title and headings helps me to know what to expect while reading."

Carl: "When I preview the pictures, I get interested in the topic."

Jack: "Predicting what's going to happen gets me more involved in the story. If my prediction is wrong, I change it."

Preview the passage and think about making a prediction. Then, read the passage.

EXPLORING A CAVE

Paula's hand trembled, causing the beam from her flashlight to wobble across the rocky walls. A steady *drip*, *drip*, *drip* echoed through the darkness.

Paula stopped and listened hard. All around her, she could hear a soft fluttering. It sounded almost like a breeze rustling leaves. Pointing her flashlight up, she looked for the source of the sound. The noise grew louder as hundreds of bats, disturbed by the light, swirled and circled in the air above Paula's head.

What do you do when you preview a text? Check the boxes that apply.

☐ Do you read the title?
☐ Do you identify the topic?
☐ Do you set a goal for reading?

How does thinking about predicting help you understand the text?

_____
_____
_____

Why might you change your prediction while you are reading?

_____
_____
_____

▶YOUR TURN

Preview "Waves From a Distant Storm" to help you make predictions. Then read the passage and answer the questions.

1. What did you do to preview the text?

2. How did making a prediction help you understand the passage?

3. Why might you change your prediction while you are reading?

4. How does thinking about predicting help you understand the text?

Waves From a Distant Storm

Brian Caldwell checked the mainsail. The 20-year-old sailor was aboard his sturdy red sloop, the *Mau Vavau*. He had just spent another **satisfying** day alone on the open sea. His journey had taken him from Hawaii to the eastern Indian Ocean. Brian was **passionate** about sailing. That passion was driving him to become the youngest sailor to voyage solo around the world.

Smooth Sailing Brian gazed up at the clear, starlit sky. The boat, whose name means "waves from a distant storm," was handling well. Brian went below deck to make his daily entry into the ship's log. Once he reached port, he would send a copy to his hometown paper. It would be published in the latest **issue**.

Everything Upside Down Around midnight, just as Brian was dozing off, a loud roar filled the air, and a giant wall of water slammed into the vessel. The monster wave turned the boat upside down. Brian was pitched from his bed. Minutes felt like hours. Finally the boat settled into

an upright position. Bruised and breathless, Brian opened the hatch. Miraculously, the main sail was still in place. Brian shook his head in disbelief that the very thing that **inspired** his boat's name had nearly destroyed them both.

Keep your reading smooth. Pause only at natural breaks between phrases.

FLUENCY

READ on your OWN
Success Stories, pages 26–28

BEFORE YOU READ

Think about what you read yesterday. What did Andrew do for his school band?

AS YOU READ

Preview pages 26–28 of "What's the Secret?"
What did you do when you previewed the pages? Check the boxes that apply.

☐ Did you read the title and headings?

☐ Did you look at the picture?

☐ Did you identify the topic?

☐ Did you think about what you already know about the topic?

☐ Did you set a goal for reading?

What do you predict you will be reading about?

_____

_____

Read pages 26–28.
Check your prediction. Did you need to change it as you were reading?

_____

How does thinking about predicting help you understand the passage?

_____

_____

VOCABULARY
Watch for the words you are learning about.

passion: something a person feels great enthusiasm for

satisfying: giving a feeling of well-being

issues: questions or problems to be solved

dedication: willingness to devote much time or energy to something

FLUENCY
Read smoothly from one paragraph to the next.

AFTER YOU READ

Choose the most interesting thing you learned about a character in this chapter and tell what you learned.

METACOGNITION: Thinking About Choosing Strategies

What Good Readers Do

Before reading
- Preview.
- Think about the topic.
- Ask questions.
- Make predictions.

During reading
- Identify the topic, main idea, and details.
- Identify text structure, ask questions, visualize, make inferences.
- Reread.

After reading
- Summarize.
- Ask questions.
- Use graphic organizers to organize information.

Learn the STRATEGY

Good readers think about which strategies to use and how these strategies will help them as they read. You have considered how summarizing, questioning, and predicting help you understand what you read. Now think about choosing two or more of these strategies together to help you understand different texts.

The Forbidden City sits right in the heart of Beijing, China. This complex of wooden buildings was built between 1406 and 1422. Fourteen emperors lived there.

The last emperor of China, Puyi, was only three years old when he became emperor. He lived in the Forbidden City surrounded by adult advisors. He did not see his brother or sister or any other child until he was seven years old, and he did not see his mother again until he was ten. Life in the Forbidden City for Puyi was empty of love.

In 1924, Puyi's dynasty was overthrown, and Puyi was forced to leave the Forbidden City. It was no longer used as a royal residence. Today, it is known as the Palace Museum. Its architecture and rich history make the Forbidden City one of China's greatest treasures.

Which strategies did you use to help you understand this passage? Check the boxes that apply.

- ☐ Summarizing
- ☐ Questioning
- ☐ Predicting

How did choosing a strategy help you better understand the text?

_____
_____
_____
_____
_____

Think about what strategies to use as you read
"The End of a Dynasty." Then answer the questions.

SOCIAL STUDIES CONNECTION

The End of a Dynasty

The Last Emperor The last of the Manchu Qing emperors came into power in 1908. Puyi became ruler when his uncle, the previous Emperor, died. Just shy of his third birthday, Puyi was the youngest Chinese emperor ever to ascend to the throne and his youth did not **inspire** confidence. In 1912, a revolution overthrew the government. A republic was established. Puyi was permitted to remain in Beijing and live in the Forbidden City. He was also allowed to keep his imperial title. However,

Puyi became emperor at the age of three.

he was no longer considered the ruler. He had to be **satisfied** with these conditions.

Life as a Regular Teenager When he was 13, Puyi started to learn about the world outside of China. He became **passionate** about life in Western countries. He realized that he was a prisoner in the Forbidden City. At the age of 15, he **voluntarily** tried to leave by bribing the guards, who took his money but then betrayed him.

Three years later in 1924, a warlord staged a coup. The warlord took over Beijing and forced Puyi to give up his imperial title and leave the Forbidden City. From this point on, Puyi was treated as a regular Chinese citizen, and he loved it. He is said to have exclaimed, "I had no freedom as emperor. Now I have found my freedom!"

1. Which strategies did you use to help you understand this passage?

2. How did choosing a strategy help you better understand the text?

To help your reading go smoother, review any words in boldfaced type before you read. Make sure you know how to pronounce these words.

FLUENCY

READ on your OWN
Success Stories, pages 29–31

BEFORE YOU READ

Think about what you read during the past few days. Which of the teens you read about impressed you the most?

AS YOU READ

Read pages 29–31 of "You Can Make a Difference!" (STOP)
Answer the questions.

Which strategies did you use to help you understand these pages?

_____
_____
_____

How did these strategies help you understand the text?

_____
_____
_____

How does choosing a strategy help you to better understand the text?

_____
_____
_____

VOCABULARY
Watch for the words you are learning about.

dedicated: willing to devote much time or energy to something

worthwhile: of real value

voluntarily: freely giving a job or service

FLUENCY
Preview the text and look up any words you have difficulty pronouncing.

AFTER YOU READ

Why do you think it's important to have goals in life?

Make Words Yours!

Learn the WORDS

Here are some words you will be reading in the next week. They are also words you need to know for your everyday reading.

WORD AND EXPLANATION	EXAMPLE	WRITE AN EXAMPLE
Something that is **fertile** is able to produce much of something else, such as crops or ideas.	We caught many fish in the **fertile** sea.	If you had **fertile** soil, what crops would you grow?
If something is **marvelous**, it is great or extraordinary.	We looked at a **marvelous** painting when we were at the museum.	What is a **marvelous** idea you've had recently?
A **myth** is a story that isn't true or an old legend that usually tries to explain something in nature.	The ancient **myth** was about why the seasons change.	Why might ancient cultures have created **myths** to try to explain thunderstorms?
The **status** of something is its condition, or where it stands.	The teacher asked what the **status** was of our project.	Why are doctors usually considered to have high **status** in society?
Something that is a **trait** is a special quality or characteristic that describes someone.	Honesty is a **trait** that people admire.	Why might fairness be a good **trait** for a judge?
Something is **unlimited** when it has no end.	We had an **unlimited** amount of money to spend on our project.	What would you like to have an **unlimited** amount of?
If you are a **vendor**, you sell something.	The street **vendor** was selling sandwiches and pretzels.	What are some other things that a **vendor** might sell?
To **yield** is to give up or to produce.	The tree **yielded** many apples this season.	What would you want a treasure hunt to **yield**?

➤YOUR TURN

Answer these questions and be ready to explain your answers.

1. Would a pilot want to know the *status* of a flight? _____

2. Is a *myth* true? _____

3. Would a *vendor* be someone you sold something to? _____

4. When we *yield*, do we give up? _____

Choose the right word

fertile	marvelous	myth	yield
status	trait	unlimited	vendor

Fill each blank with the correct word.

5. Tom did a great job. _____

6. Sue is honest. _____

7. Iva told an old story about why the sun rises and sets. _____

8. The citizens will not give up their right to vote. _____

9. My report is due tomorrow and I have finished it. _____

10. They offered us as many supplies as we needed. _____

11. The soil was rich and we grew many crops last year. _____

12. The craft fair is full of booths and people selling things. _____

Show that you know the words. Write about inventors.

Show that you know

Complete the sentences.

13. A *marvelous* invention an inventor made is

14. An inventor should have a *fertile* mind because

15. Some *traits* of inventors are

16. If I had *unlimited* money, I would try to invent

READ on your OWN
Success Stories, pages 32–35

BEFORE YOU READ

Think about what you already know about scientific discoveries.
What are some ways that people make scientific discoveries?

AS YOU READ

Preview pages 32–35 of "Right Under Your Nose."
Answer the questions.

What did you do to preview the passage?

_____

_____

What·do you predict you will be reading about?

_____

_____

Read pages 32–35.
Answer the questions.

What questions did you have before, during, and after you read?

_____

_____

What did you do to help you prepare to summarize what you read?

_____

_____

AFTER YOU READ

Choose the most interesting section or page. What is one new fact you learned?

VOCABULARY
Watch for the words you are learning about.

marvelous: great, or worth wondering about

unlimited: going on without end

FLUENCY
Read with expression, vary the volume and tone of your voice.

METACOGNITION: Thinking About Text Structure

What Good Readers Do

Before reading
- Preview.
- Think about the topic.
- Ask questions.
- Make predictions.

During reading
- Identify the topic, main idea, and details.
- Identify text structure, ask questions, visualize, make inferences.
- Reread.

After reading
- Summarize.
- Ask questions.
- Use graphic organizers to organize information.

Learn the STRATEGY

You know that all texts have structure. Think about the different structures of expository, or nonfiction, texts you read. These structures are description, sequence, comparison-contrast, problem-solution, and cause-and-effect.

One class discussed what they thought about before they read expository texts in order to identify a text structure. They also discussed how graphic organizers helped them organize information during and after they read. Here are their ideas:

If you're reading...	It's probably...	You can write important details...
a social studies article about a group of people and how they live,	**description** because it describes a topic and gives detailed information about it.	in an idea web.
a science article about how to do something,	**sequence** because it lists a series of things in order.	in a timeline or a flowchart.
an article that discusses what happens as a result of something,	**cause-and-effect** because it explains how one thing causes another thing to happen.	in a cause-and-effect chart.

What steps do you go through to identify the text structure of a passage?

_____

_____

_____

Why is thinking about the text structure of a passage helpful?

_____

_____

_____

Read the first paragraph of "A Seed of an Idea," and think about its text structure. Then read the passage and answer the questions.

1. What did you do to identify the text structure of the passage?

2. What helped you identify the text structure?

3. Why is thinking about the text structure of the passage helpful?

A SEED OF AN IDEA

Kavita Shukla was worried. The teenage girl was visiting family in India, and the last thing she needed was an upset stomach. Yet that's just what she was likely to get after mistakenly swallowing germ-laden water while brushing her teeth. Her grandmother offered Kavita some fenugreek seeds to keep her from becoming sick. The herb had strong medicinal powers, she told Kavita.

Sure enough, the fenugreek worked and Kavita had an illness-free visit. On the way home, she thought about the fenugreek. The plant's seeds did indeed seem to have **marvelous** curative powers. She wondered if the fenugreek plant had other useful applications.

One day, Kavita noticed that some strawberries in her refrigerator had spoiled. She thought again of the fenugreek. It had kept her from getting sick from germs. Could it keep food from getting spoiled? Kavita decided to try wrapping food in packaging paper made with fenugreek seeds. She conducted experiments to see how well the paper kept food fresh. Sure enough, Kavita's **questing** had helped her find a way to keep food fresh!

Kavita was awarded a patent for her new invention and was able to find a **vendor** to mass produce and sell her packaging paper. Kavita is excited and happy to have created something useful. Her story is a reminder that there are **unlimited** opportunities for new discoveries. All you need is an inquisitive mind and a little imagination.

Vary your expression as you read to make your reading sound smoother and more interesting.

FLUENCY

READ on your OWN
Success Stories, pages 36–38

BEFORE YOU READ

Think about the section you read before. How was gold first discovered in the United States?

AS YOU READ

Read pages 36–38.
Answer the questions.

What did you do to identify the text structure of the pages?

_____

_____

What helped you identify the text structure?

_____

_____

What kind of graphic organizer could you use to organize information?

_____

_____

Why is thinking about the text structure of a passage and using a graphic organizer helpful?

_____

_____

AFTER YOU READ

Choose a page and tell the most interesting thing you learned from it.

Get Wordwise!
The Suffixes -ous, -ology, and -or

Learn More About the WORDS

As you know, **suffixes** are word endings. Suffixes sometimes change the part of speech of a word.

The suffix **-ous** means full of. The new word is an adjective.

The suffix **-ology** means the study or science of. The new word is a noun.

The suffix **-or** is similar to the suffix -er in that both mean a person who. The new word is a noun.

Learning suffixes can help you understand the meanings of words you hear and read.

WORD AND EXPLANATION	WORD WITH SUFFIX	WRITE AN EXAMPLE
An **adventure** is an exciting experience that can sometimes be dangerous.	If someone is **adventurous**, that person is full of adventure and likes to take risks.	What is something **adventurous** that you would like to do?
A **marvel** is something that is astonishing or wonderful.	If something is **marvelous**, it is full of marvel and is great.	What is something **marvelous** that has happened to you?
A **myth** is a story that isn't true or an old legend that usually tries to explain something in nature.	**Mythology** is the study of myths.	Why might someone have an interest in **mythology**?
To **vend** is to sell something.	A **vendor** is someone who sells something.	Where might you find a **vendor**?

▶YOUR TURN

Which word makes sense?

Circle the correct word in each pair.

1. We had a **marvel / marvelous** time at the party.

2. The eclipse was a **marvel / marvelous** rarely seen.

3. We didn't know what an **adventure / adventurous** it would be to go boating at night.

4. Jim is **adventure / adventurous** and wants to go on an African safari.

5. The **vend / vendor** was selling watches.

6. I will **vend / vendor** my crafts at the fair.

7. Jacque told a **myth / mythology** about how birds learned to fly.

8. The stories found in Greek **myth / mythology** are exciting.

Choose the right suffix

-or -ous -ology

Fill each blank with a new word. Create the new word by adding a suffix from the box to the word in parentheses.

9. **(myth)** I read about Helios, the sun god in Greek _____.

10. **(vend)** We bought an ice-cream cone from the _____.

11. **(marvel)** The children loved the _____ story.

12. **(adventure)** The storm made our usual walk home _____.

Show that you know about words with suffixes. Use them to write about something that interests you.

Show that you know

adventurous   marvelous   mythology   vendor

Write two sentences. In each, use one of the words from the box.

13. _____

_____

14. _____

_____

_____

READ on your OWN
Success Stories, pages 39–42

BEFORE YOU READ

Think about what you read the past few days. Why did Mel Fisher want to find the *Atocha*?

AS YOU READ

Read pages 39–42 of "Accidental Archaeology."
Answer the questions.

What did you do to identify the text structure of the pages?

_____

What helped you identify the text structure?

_____

_____

_____

What kind of graphic organizer could you use to organize information?

_____

Why is thinking about the text structure of a passage and using a graphic organizer helpful?

_____

_____

_____

VOCABULARY
Watch for the words you are learning about.

myth: a fable, or a story that isn't true

yield: to give or give up

trait: a characteristic or quality that describes something about someone

status: the position of people or things in relation to each other

FLUENCY
Use tone and expression to emphasize important parts in a text.

AFTER YOU READ

Choose the part of this section you think is most interesting and retell it.

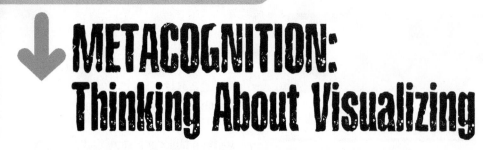

METACOGNITION: Thinking About Visualizing

What Good Readers Do

Before reading
• Preview.
• Think about the topic.
• Ask questions.
• Make predictions.

During reading
• Identify the topic, main idea, and details.
• Identify text structure, ask questions, visualize, make inferences.
• Reread.

After reading
• Summarize.
• Ask questions.
• Use graphic organizers to organize information.

Learn the STRATEGY

Good readers think about creating pictures in their minds when they read. Visualizing helps them understand what they read. Good readers visualize in different ways.

• Toni says, "I look at the illustrations to help me picture what I read."
• Jackson says, "I look for words that describe things. I know I need to stop more often and make a picture in my mind."
• Annie says, "When I read directions, I make a mental picture of what happens first, next, and last. I also like to draw graphic organizers to help me see how ideas relate to one another."

Archaeologists primarily study human activity from past civilizations. However, they do not work alone. They rely on other specialists to help them. For example, in order to learn about the diets of ancient people, they talk to experts on plants and animals. These experts can tell them about the types of plants and animals that were common to the region in earlier times. The information provided by other scientists is vital. Their knowledge can help archaeologists draw accurate conclusions about the people and places they study.

What did you do to visualize what you read? Check the boxes that apply.

☐ Did you picture a sequence of events?
☐ Did you make a graphic organizer?

How does visualizing help you better understand what you read?

_____
_____
_____
_____

Read "Of Sea and Sand" and think about visualizing the island and the submerged forest.

1. What did you do to visualize what you read? Check the boxes that apply.
- ☐ Did you look at the illustration?
- ☐ Did you make mental images based on sensory words?
- ☐ Did you picture a sequence of events?
- ☐ Did you make a graphic organizer?

2. How were these steps useful in visualizing?

3. How does thinking about visualizing help you better understand the text?

Of Sea and Sand

Researcher Alistair Rennie had heard of a forest buried deep beneath the beaches of Sanday Island, Orkney. Was this story just a **myth**? Could there possibly be ancient trees hidden under the sands of this small island just off the coast of Scotland? Mr. Rennie decided to investigate. He found nineteenth-century writings that told of mysterious black moss that appeared on the windswept beaches after a storm. A sea captain's old map showed where a submerged forest was thought to exist.

Mr. Rennie and his work crew began to dig holes along the beach at Sanday Island. Their first few attempts didn't **yield** anything. Finally, the crew excavated peat, a type of moss. Entangled in the peat were parts of trees. Samples were sent to Glasgow University, where their **traits** could be analyzed. Sure enough, the analysis revealed that the trees were a type of willow. The samples were actually 6,500 years old!

Mr. Rennie concluded that the sea level had risen and covered land that once was a forest. The island appeared to be sinking. Its current **status**, however, was not in jeopardy. The rate at which the sea was rising was quite slow. In the past 6,500 years, the water had risen only about 10 feet.

Keep up your pace to maintain interest. Explain events as if you were a part of them.

FLUENCY

READ on your OWN
Success Stories, pages 43–45

BEFORE YOU READ

Think about the section you read before. Why is the Lascaux cave closed to tourists today?

AS YOU READ

Read pages 43–45 of "Famous Young Fossil Finders."
Answer the questions.

What did you do to visualize what you read?
Give examples for all that apply.

☐ I looked at illustrations or photographs. Example:
_____

☐ I found descriptive words. Example: _____

☐ I made mental images based on sensory words. Example:
_____

☐ I pictured a sequence of events. Example: _____

How does thinking about visualizing help you better understand the text?

_____

_____

VOCABULARY
Watch for the words you are learning about.

traits: characteristics or qualities that describe something about someone

marvelous: great, or worth wondering about

yield: to give or give up

status: the position of people or things in relation to each other

FLUENCY
Think about how the people are feeling, and try to convey that in your tone and expression.

AFTER YOU READ

What would you do if you found a fossil?

Metacognition: Thinking About Choosing Strategies

What Good Readers Do

Before reading
- Preview.
- Think about the topic.
- Ask questions.
- Make predictions.

During reading
- Identify the topic, main idea, and details.
- Identify text structure, ask questions, visualize, make inferences.
- Reread.

After reading
- Summarize.
- Ask questions.
- Use graphic organizers to organize information.

Learn the STRATEGY

Good readers know when they are not understanding what they read. When they are not understanding, they stop reading. They think about which strategies they can use to help them understand. Then they reread trying different strategies until they know they understand the text.

You have considered how summarizing, questioning, predicting, text structure, and visualizing help you understand what you read. Now think about how you could use two or more of these strategies together to help you understand what you read.

Read the paragraph and answer the questions.

On a fine September day in 1940, four friends set out on a hike through a forest south of Montignac, France. Simon's dog, Robot, scampered ahead. Between the trees, the boys could see Robot running up Lascaux Hill. The four friends were too busy having a good time to pay attention to the dog. Then, when Simon's whistles and calls went unanswered, they realized that Robot was lost. They frantically searched the hillside and found a dark hole in the ground. Poor Robot had fallen through the hole to a cave far below. The boys descended into the cave to rescue Robot. They couldn't believe what they found in the cave.

Which strategies did you use to help you understand this passage? Check the boxes that apply.

☐ Summarizing
☐ Questioning
☐ Predicting
☐ Text structure
☐ Visualizing

Why did you choose these strategies?

_____
_____
_____
_____
_____

YOUR TURN

**Think about what strategies to use as you read "Prehistoric Art."
Then answer the questions.**

Prehistoric Art

The Lascaux Cave The Bordeaux region of France has many caves. Some of these caves contain fine examples of prehistoric art. Striking paintings have been found in the Cave of Lascaux. The cave was discovered in 1940 by four boys on a hike. It features some of the best preserved cave paintings ever discovered.

The images show animals being hunted. These scenes suggest how important hunting was to people of this era. Bison, bulls, and horses are drawn with amazing detail. One image, known as the Large Bull, is beautifully drawn. The **marvelous** brushwork gives the bull a soft lifelike appearance.

Cave paintings showed animals in amazing detail.

Preserving the Images One of the reasons for the paintings' outstanding condition is that the cave had remained undiscovered for so long. The entrance was overgrown with plants and weeds. These plants had prevented air outside the cave from mixing with air inside it. As a result, the air within the cave did not build up moisture. Moisture would have ruined the images.

Many visitors went to the cave after its discovery. However, the **unlimited** traffic caused concern that the paintings would be ruined. The French government closed the cave to the public in 1963 to prevent further damage from occurring.

1. Which strategies did you use to help you understand this passage?

2. How did these strategies help you understand what you read?

Find ways to read an informational passage in an engaging way. Use expression to highlight points that are interesting or amusing.

FLUENCY

READ on your OWN
Success Stories, pages 46–48

BEFORE YOU READ

Think about the last pages you read. What important discoveries did Mary Anning make?

AS YOU READ

Read pages 46–48 of "Accidental Discoveries in Science."
Answer the questions.

Which strategies did you use to help you understand these pages? Check the boxes that apply.

☐ Summarizing

☐ Questioning

☐ Predicting

☐ Text structure

☐ Visualizing

Why did you choose these strategies?

_____

_____

_____

How did these strategies help you understand the text?

_____

_____

_____

AFTER YOU READ

Choose the scientific discovery you are most interested in. Explain why you are interested in it.

Make Words Yours!

Learn the WORDS

As you read more about inventions, you'll come across these words. This is your chance to get to know them better.

WORD AND EXPLANATION	EXAMPLE	WRITE AN EXAMPLE
A **debut** is the first time a person or thing appears in public.	The young singer made her **debut** in a concert hall in New York City.	When have you made a **debut**?
If something is a **pitfall**, it is a hidden danger or problem.	One **pitfall** of being famous is that you have little privacy.	What is one **pitfall** of winning a lot of money?
When you **propose** something, you present a plan for others to consider.	I **propose** that our environmental club plant five trees on the school grounds.	What changes might you **propose** for your classroom?
Something that is a **remainder** is left over.	Juan Carlos gave the **remainder** of his sandwich to the dog.	After school, what do you do with the **remainder** of your day?
Something that is **stellar** is outstanding.	Anna made a **stellar** discovery of a complete dinosaur skull.	Who do you think gave a **stellar** performance in a recent movie?
A **succession** is a group of people or things that comes or happens one after the other.	A **succession** of hot, sunny days made our vacation wonderful.	What are some other things that might happen in **succession**?
Technology is the systematic use of science to solve problems. People often think of electronic products, like computers, as technology.	**Technology** has made our lives easier by helping us with new inventions.	What has **technology** improved?
If something is **vivid**, it is bright, strong, and clear. Colors, dreams, and memories can be **vivid**.	The **vivid** color of the flowers attracted the bees.	What are other things with **vivid** colors?

►YOUR TURN

Decide whether each statement is true or false. Be ready to explain your answers.

1. *Vivid* colors are dull. _____

2. When you make a *debut*, it is the second time you do something. _____

3. A *remainder* is extra. _____

4. Things done in *succession* are done out of order. _____

Choose the right word

> debut   pitfall   remainder   propose
> vivid   stellar   succession   technology

Fill each blank with the correct word.

5. We will [_____] our plan at the meeting.

6. We put away the [_____] of the chairs.

7. They used computers and other [_____], so the invention worked well.

8. A [_____] of baking cookies is that you want to eat them.

9. The [_____] of the young band was at the school dance.

10. The painting's [_____] colors made it very interesting.

11. There was a [_____] of drummers in the marching band.

12. Vanessa's [_____] speech won the debate contest.

> Show that you know the words by writing about inventions.

Show that you know

Complete the sentences.

13. A *pitfall* an inventor might come across is _____

14. *Technology* is important in inventions because _____

15. An invention I would like to *propose* is _____

16. A recent *stellar* invention is _____

READ on your OWN
Success Stories, pages 49–51

BEFORE YOU READ

Think about what you just read. How did Alexander Fleming discover penicillin?

AS YOU READ

Read pages 49–51 of "Accidental Inventions."
Answer the questions.

Which strategies did you use to help you understand these pages?
Check the boxes that apply.

☐ Summarizing

☐ Questioning

☐ Predicting

☐ Text structure

☐ Visualizing

Why did you choose these strategies?

_____

_____

_____

How did the strategies help you understand the text?

_____

_____

_____

VOCABULARY
Watch for the words you are learning about.

succession: a series of events that come right after one another

technology: a way of accomplishing a task, using specialized knowledge or methods

debut: the first appearance of something

FLUENCY
Read at an even pace as if you were telling the story yourself.

AFTER YOU READ

If you were trying to invent something, what would you invent?

METACOGNITION: Thinking About Inferring

What Good Readers Do

Before reading
- Preview.
- Think about the topic.
- Ask questions.
- Make predictions.

During reading
- Identify the topic, main idea, and details.
- Identify text structure, ask questions, visualize, make inferences.
- Reread.

After reading
- Summarize.
- Ask questions.
- Use graphic organizers to organize information.

Learn the STRATEGY

When you infer, you think about things in the text that the writer did not say directly. Good readers think about how they can make inferences about what they read so that they will better understand. They think about connecting things in the text to things they already know. They think about connecting different ideas in the text. They also connect events or people in the text to their lives and their feelings.

Nikola Tesla was a brilliant inventor. One of his inventions made it possible to deliver electricity over wires for long distances. He also was a pioneer in wireless communication.

Tesla began his career as an inventor at a young age. At five years old, he designed a motor powered by insects. He glued June bugs to the blades of a small propeller. As the bugs flapped their wings, the propeller turned. Unfortunately, one of Tesla's playmates had an appetite for bugs. The other boy convinced Tesla to eat the bugs. The motor was abandoned when the young inventor and his friend became sick.

What kinds of inferences did you make? Check the box or boxes that apply.

- ☐ I connected two different ideas in this text.
- ☐ I connected the text to my life and feelings.
- ☐ I connected the events in the text to things that I already know.

How did inferring help you understand the text?

_____

_____

_____

➤ YOUR TURN

Read "Beautiful and Brilliant." Then answer the questions.

1. What did you do to make an inference? Check the boxes that apply.
   - ☐ I related this text to something else I've read.
   - ☐ I related the people in the text to people I know.
   - ☐ I related the events in the text to things that have happened in the world.

2. How did thinking about inferring help you understand the text?
   - ☐ It prepared me to think about what the author said and didn't say.
   - ☐ It prepared me to make connections and decisions about the text. It got me involved in my reading.
   - ☐ It helped me to evaluate what I thought the author meant but didn't say.

Read the text at a relaxed pace as if you were telling a story.

FLUENCY

Beautiful *and* Brilliant

Cell phones and wireless communications utilize a special **technology** called "spread spectrum." This concept was **proposed** during World War II by a famous Hollywood actress and a composer. Hedy Lamarr, a beautiful star of the 1940s, and composer George Antheil came up with a secret communications system. This system was based on the same principle that operated old-time player pianos. A player piano holds and changes notes to make a melody. In a similar way, spread spectrum holds and changes radio frequencies to send messages. Frequencies are switched in rapid **succession**. The synchronized changes allow messages to be sent without being detected. Secrecy is guaranteed.

The system was intended for World War II submarines. It actually made its **debut** many years later. The military found it a highly effective way to communicate. In recent years, spread spectrum technology has seen more widespread use. Wireless computer networks, fax machines, and cell phones all utilize this **technology**.

Lamarr and Antheil never received any money for their invention. They had donated the patent as part of the war effort. However, they have received belated awards acknowledging their scientific contribution. In 1997, they were given the Electronic Frontier Foundation (EFF) Pioneer Award. Their invention led the way to modern **technology**.

The invention that actress Hedy Lamarr helped create is used in cell phones and other modern devices.

READ on your OWN
Success Stories, pages 52–54

BEFORE YOU READ

Think about what you just read. What did Charles Goodyear do to make rubber useful?

AS YOU READ

Read pages 52–54 of "Everyday Inventions."
Answer the questions.

What did you do to make an inference?

_____

_____

_____

_____

How did inferring help you understand the text?

_____

_____

_____

_____

_____

VOCABULARY
Watch for the words you are learning about.

pitfall: a danger that isn't easy to recognize

debut: the first appearance of something

succession: a series of events that come one after another

vivid: bright or intense

technology: a way of accomplishing a task using specialized knowledge or methods

FLUENCY
Practice reading long sentences so you can read them at an even pace.

AFTER YOU READ

What do you think is the most useful, simple invention? Why?

Get Wordwise!
Word Origins

Learn More About the WORDS

Many English words can be traced back to other languages such as French, Spanish, Latin, and Greek. When you trace a word back to the original word and meaning in its own language, you find its origin. **Word origins** help us understand and remember what English words mean. The word *myth* comes from the Greek word *mythos*, which means speech, thought, or story. The word *myth* has a similar meaning in English. *Myth* means an old legend or story that usually tries to explain something in nature.

WORD AND ORIGIN	EXPLANATION	WRITE AN EXAMPLE
Debut comes from the French word *debut*, which is the first move in a game such as bowling.	**Debut** is the first time a person or a thing appears in public. I made my acting _____ when I was just 6 years old.	If you were making your acting **debut**, what show would you want to be on?
Stellar comes from the Latin word *stella*, meaning a star.	**Stellar** describes something that is outstanding. Leo won first prize for his _____ painting.	In your opinion, what kind of day is **stellar**?
Succession comes from the Latin word *successio*, meaning to follow after.	A **succession** is a group of people or things that come one after the other. We had a _____ of tasty meals.	How do you feel after a **succession** of rainy days?
Technology comes from the Greek word *technologia*, meaning systematic treatment of art or craft.	**Technology** is the systematic use of science to solve problems. Cordless phones are an example of a way _____ has changed phones.	What is another way **technology** has changed phones?
Vivid comes from the Latin word *vivere*, meaning to live.	Something is **vivid** when it is bright, strong, and clear. I thought my _____ dream was real.	What is a **vivid** memory you have from your childhood?

►YOUR TURN

Choose the right word

> debut   stellar   succession   technology   vivid

Fill each blank with the correct word from the box.

1. The remarkable advances in _____ have made it much easier to get information.

2. Kate had some _____ ideas for the project that I knew would work.

3. The _____ of Sean's invention is planned for next year.

4. A _____ of new computer models has come out quickly over the years.

5. The photographs are extremely _____ and look like the real thing.

What is the word origin?

Fill each blank with the correct word from the box above and the word origin.

6. The _____ of the telephone changed communication forever.

7. Cell phone _____ had its beginnings as an idea for sending secret messages during war.

8. Don's _____ performance in the play earned him an acting award.

9. The artist used such _____ colors that his work stood out from others.

10. The marching band used a _____ of steps and turns that impressed the judges.

> Show that you know about word origins. Write about how these words are the same.

Show that you know

Answer the questions. Use sentences.

11. How is the meaning of the English word *debut* similar to the French word *debut*?

12. How is the meaning of the English word *stellar* similar to the Latin word *stella*?

READ on your OWN
Success Stories, pages 55–57

BEFORE YOU READ

Think about what you just read. How did George de Mestral invent Velcro®?

AS YOU READ

Read pages 55–57 of "Striking It Rich in Unexpected Places." (STOP)
Answer the questions.

What did you do to make an inference?

_____

_____

_____

How did inferring help you understand the text?

_____

_____

_____

VOCABULARY
Watch for the words you are learning about.

remainder: something that is left after the rest has been taken away

stellar: outstanding

pitfall: a danger that isn't easy to recognize

vivid: bright or intense

FLUENCY
Read at an even pace and pay attention to appropriate places to pause and take breaths.

AFTER YOU READ

Choose something that happened in this section that you think is funny and explain it.

METACOGNITION: Knowing Which Strategy to Use

What Good Readers Do

Before reading
- Preview.
- Think about the topic.
- Ask questions.
- Make predictions.

During reading
- Identify the topic, main idea, and details.
- Identify text structure, ask questions, visualize, make inferences.
- Reread.

After reading
- Summarize.
- Ask questions.
- Use graphic organizers to organize information.

Learn the STRATEGY

Good readers think about what is going on in their mind as they are reading. When they are not understanding what they read, they know to stop reading. Then they think about using different strategies to help them understand the text.

You have considered how summarizing, questioning, predicting, text structure, visualizing, and inferring help you understand what you read. By carefully thinking about each strategy, you will know which strategies to use and when to use them.

Read the paragraph below and think about which strategies will help you understand it.

Necessity is the mother of invention. Necessity inspired Albert J. Parkerhouse to invent the first wire coat hanger in 1903. Parkerhouse worked at a wire and novelty company in Jackson, Michigan. He grew tired of listening to his coworkers complain about a shortage of coat hooks. He solved the problem using the materials he had. He joined two pieces of wire together to form an oval, then he twisted the ends to make a hook. Parkerhouse's coat hanger was such a success he obtained a patent for it.

Which strategies did you use to help you understand this passage? Check the boxes that apply.

☐ Summarizing
☐ Questioning
☐ Predicting
☐ Text structure
☐ Visualizing
☐ Inferring

How did knowing which strategies to use help you understand the text?

_____
_____
_____
_____

YOUR TURN

Read "Close Observation" and answer the questions.

....
1. Which strategies did you use to help you understand this passage?

....
2. Why did you choose these strategies?

....
3. How did knowing which strategies to use help you understand the text?

CLOSE Observation

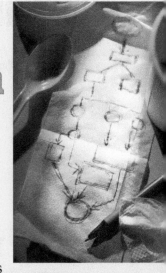

Some inventors rely on their imaginations to come up with the perfect design. Others simply use nature as their model. Still other people discover solutions to problems completely by accident.

Clarence Birdseye made an interesting observation. Birdseye was working in Canada during the winter of 1915. His native Inuit guides went fishing often. They set the **remainder** of the fish that they did not eat out to freeze in the bitter cold. The fish were kept frozen for months, but this method was not a **pitfall**. Birdseye noticed that when the fish were thawed and cooked, they tasted as fresh as when they were just caught. Birdseye returned home and **proposed** using the same process with other foods. He carefully worked with scientists to design a quick-freeze method for keeping meats and vegetables fresh indefinitely.

Inspiration struck Swiss engineer Georges de Mestral. In 1948, he returned from a walk and noticed burrs stuck to his clothing. He put the burrs under a microscope and studied their structure. Tiny barbs caused the burrs to stick to the looped fibers in his clothing. The finding inspired de Mestral to design a fastener based on the burr's design. The **stellar** new fastener came to be known as Velcro®.

Reread the passage in segments. Pause and use pacing to show the transition between segments.

FLUENCY

READ on your OWN
Success Stories, pages 58–60

BEFORE YOU READ

Think about what you just read. How was an old copy of the Declaration of Independence found at a flea market?

AS YOU READ

Read pages 58–60 of "Treasures at School."
Answer the questions.

Which strategies did you use to help you understand these pages? Check the boxes that apply.

☐ Summarizing

☐ Questioning

☐ Predicting

☐ Text structure

☐ Visualizing

☐ Inferring

Why did you choose these strategies?

_____

_____

How did knowing which strategies to use help you understand the text?

_____

_____

_____

AFTER YOU READ

What discovery or invention would you like to make? Why?

VOCABULARY
Watch for the words you are learning about.

remainder: something that is left after the rest has been taken away

vivid: bright or intense

propose: to present a plan for consideration

FLUENCY
Preview the text for natural breaks so you can read with a natural pacing.

Unit 7 Reflection

VOCABULARY

The easiest part of learning new words is

The hardest part is

I still need to work on

Success Stories

COMPREHENSION

Thinking about how and when I use the strategies of summarizing, questioning, predicting, text structure, visualizing, and inferring helps me when I read because

Thinking about how I use different strategies can be hard because

FLUENCY

I read most fluently when

I still need to work on

INDEPENDENT READING

My favorite part of Success Stories is

A

abandon (uh-BAN-duhn) to give something up, or leave it

adventure (ad-VEHN-chuhr) an exciting experience that can sometimes be dangerous. **Adventurous** (ad-VEHN-chuh-ruhs) describes someone who is full of adventure and likes to take risks.

amid (uh-MIHD) surrounded by something, or in the middle of it

ancestor (AN-sehs-tuhr) a person you are descended from, such as your grandparents and great-grandparents

arrange (uh-RAYNJ) to put things in a certain order. **Arranging** (uh-RAYN-jihng) means putting things in a certain order. An **arrangement** (uh-RAYNJ-muhnt) is something put together in a certain way.

attitude (A-tuh-tood) the way you act, or behave, that shows how you are feeling

available (uh-VAY-luh-buhl) ready for use, or easy to get

awareness (uh-WEHR-nehs) knowing about something and keeping it in mind. To be **aware** (uh-WEHR) means to know about something and keep it in mind.

B

bulk (BUHLK) the biggest part of something

bystander (BY-stan-duhr) a person who watches an activity without taking part in it

C

characteristics (kehr-ihk-tuh-RIHS-tihks) the things that make a person different from someone else

circuit (SUHR-kuht) the path of an electric current

clarity (KLEHR-uh-tee) being clear or easy to understand

code (KOHD) a set of rules; a system of words or symbols used to keep a message secret

conclude (kuhn-KLOOD) to form an opinion or make a decision about something after careful thinking; to end. **Concluding** (kuhn-KLOO-dihng) means finishing. A **conclusion** (kuhn-KLOO-zhuhn) brings something to a close.

consolation (kahn-suh-LAY-shuhn) something that comforts you and makes you feel better

conspicuously (kuhn-spih-KYOO-wuhs-lee) acting in a way that brings attention

consultation (kahn-suhl-TAY-shuhn) a meeting in which someone is seeking information or advice

continue (kuhn-TIHN-yoo) to keep on doing something

D

debris (duh-BREE) the remains of something that has been destroyed

debut (DAY-byoo) the first time a person or thing appears in public

decrease (dih-KREES) to become or make less or smaller

dedicate (DEH-duh-kayt) to give attention, time, and effort to something you think is important

dependent (dih-PEHN-duhnt) relying on someone or something for help

destination (dehs-tuh-NAY-shuhn) where someone or something is going; the end of a trip. **Destiny** (DEHS-tuh-nee) is what is sure to happen in the future or something that you are meant to do. If you are **destined** (DEHS-tihnd) to do something, it seems certain that you will do it in the future.

diminish (duh-MIH-nihsh) to gradually become less or smaller

disarranged (dihs-uh-RAYNJD) out of order

discontinue (dihs-kuhn-TIHN-yoo) to stop doing or making something

dispossessed (dihs-puh-ZEHST) had your things taken away

dwelling (DWEH-lihng) a house, or a place where people live

E

elaborate (ih-LA-buh-ruht) complicated or with a lot of detail

elevated (EH-luh-VAY-tuhd) raised above the ground or another surface

encounter (ihn-KOWN-tuhr) to unexpectedly meet or come upon someone or something

enlarge (ihn-LARJ) to make something bigger

error (ER-uhr) a mistake

established (ih-STA-blishd) set up or set firmly into place

excess (EHK-sehs) too much of something. **Excessive** (ehk-SEH-sihv) means too much.

F

fatigue (fuh-TEEG) extreme tiredness or weariness

feat (FEET) an act that shows great courage, skill, or strength

federal (FEH-duh-ruhl) managed or required by the national government

feet (FEET) the plural form of the word *foot*; your **feet** are part of your body

fertile (FUHR-tihl) able to produce much of something else, such as crops or ideas

filter (FIHL-tuhr) a device that removes or separates dirt or other unwanted things from liquids or gases

findings (FYN-dihngs) what you learn or discover from doing an investigation or research

flourish (FLUHR-ihsh) to do well, grow, or be successful

formation (for-MAY-shuhn) something that is made or develops into a particular shape; the beginning or development of something; the act of making, or shaping; an arrangement of people or things for a purpose

frequency (FREE-kwehn-see) how often something repeats, or happens again and again; something that happens often; how often something happens within a set amount of time; a measure of sound waves or electricity

funding (FUHN-dihng) money given to a certain project or purpose. A **fund** (FUHND) is money set aside for a special reason. To **fund** is to put aside money for a special reason.

G

guarantee (ger-uhn-TEE) a promise that something will be done

H

heed (HEED) to pay attention to something

heritage (HER-uh-tihj) traditions that have been handed down from past generations

hoax (HOHKS) a trick to make people believe something is real that is not

hover (HUH-vuhr) to float or hang in the air over something

I

immovable (ih-MOO-vuh-buhl) cannot be moved from one place to another

import (ihm-PAWRT) something brought into one country from another to be sold

independent (ihn-duh-PEHN-duhnt) not relying on someone or something for help

inflate (ihn-FLAYT) to make larger by adding air

input (IHN-puht) to contribute, or put in something, such as data or ideas. **Input** is a contribution.

inquire (ihn-KWYUHR) to ask about something

insincere (ihn-sihn-SIHR) not honest or genuine

inspire (ihn-SPYR) to motivate or create a strong desire to do something good

intensity (ihn-TEHNT-suh-tee) great concentration or strength

interval (IHN-tuhr-vuhl) a space between things or a time between events

irretrievable (ihr-ih-TREE-vuh-buhl) not able to get and bring back

issue (ih-SHYOO) a subject or problem that people need to talk about. To **issue** means to give or supply something to someone.

L

laboratory (LA-bruh-tawr-ee) a special room or place where scientists do tests or experiments

laborious (luh-BAWR-ee-uhs) involving a lot of hard work

latter (LA-tuhr) the second of two options

lessen (LEH-sehn) to reduce or make something less

lesson (LEH-suhn) something to be taught or studied

loom (LOOM) to appear very large or threatening

M

majority (muh-JAWR-uh-tee) more than half of the people or things in a group

marvelous (MAHRV-uh-luhs) great or extraordinary. A **marvel** (MAHR-vuhl) is something astonishing or wonderful.

moderate (MAH-duh-ruht) mild, not great or extreme

movable (MOO-vuh-buhl) can be moved from one place to another

mutual (MYOO-chuh-wuhl) having the same feelings about something as someone else does

myth (MIHTH) a story that isn't true or an old legend that usually tries to explain something in nature. **Mythology** (mih-THAH-luh-jee) is the study of myths.

N

neighborhood (NAY-buhr-hood) an area of homes

nutritious (nyoo-TRIH-shuhs) healthful and good for you

O

obscure (ahb-SKYAWR) unclear, hard to see through, or difficult to understand. **Obscurity** (ahb-SKYAWR-uh-tee) means hard to find.

P

passionate (PA-shuh-nuht) showing strong feelings or emotions, such as anger or love

pinpoint (PIHN-pawnt) to find the exact place and time of something

pitfall (PIHT-fawl) a hidden danger or problem

plea (PLEE) a strong request for help

plight (PLYT) an unfortunate or difficult situation

portion (PAWR-shuhn) part of something

possess (puh-ZEHS) to have or own something

prearrange (pree-uh-RAYNJ) to put things in a certain order in advance

propose (pruh-PROHZ) to present a plan for others to consider

prosper (PRAHS-puhr) to do well, especially in earning money

pursue (puhr-SOO) to follow or chase something in order to catch it

Q

qualify (KWAH-leh-fy) to complete what is needed to do something, like enter a competition. **Qualifications** (kwah-luh-fuh-KAY-shuhns) are requirements that must be met in order to do a job or enter a competition.

quality (KWAH-luh-tee) a characteristic or a feature that make something what it is

quest (KWEHST) a long search for something

question (KWEHS-chuhn) a sentence used to ask for information

quote (KWOHT) to restate someone's exact words

R

radical (RA-dih-kuhl) very drastic or extreme

rearrange (ree-uh-RAYNJ) to put things in order again

reason (REE-zuhn) thinking through something in a logical way. **Reasonable** (REEZ-uhn-uh-buhl) means sensible or logical. **Reasonably** (REEZ-uhn-uh-blee) means in a fair or sensible way.

rebel (rih-BEHL) to resist authority or something that tries to control you

recommend (reh-kuh-MEHND) to strongly suggest or advise

refresh (rih-FREHSH) to make something or someone feel stronger, more energetic, or almost like new; to awaken or stir up; to update an image on a Web site.

relate (rih-LAYT) to connect or to make a connection

relic (REH-lihk) something that has survived from a long time ago

rely (rih-LY) to depend on someone or something

remainder (rih-MAYN-duhr) the rest of something that is left over

repossess (rih-puh-ZEHS) to take back something

request (rih-KWEHST) the act of asking for something politely

reserve (rih-ZERV) to set something aside for later use

restore (rih-STAWR) to bring something back to its original condition

retain (rih-TAYN) to keep something

retrieve (rih-TREEV) to get something and bring it back. **Retrievable** (rih-TREE-vuh-buhl) means able to get and bring back.

revision (rih-VIH-zhuhn) a change to something, usually for the better

root (ROOT) the underground part of a plant

route (ROOT) a road or course that someone travels

rural (RAWR-uhl) located in the country. **Rurally** (RAWR-uh-lee) means in the country.

S

satisfying (SA-tuhs-fy-ihng) giving a person pleasure and meeting his or her needs or wishes

scanning (SKA-nihng) looking over something quickly

scant (SKANT) barely enough of something

seclude (sih-KLOOD) to remove or separate from others. Something that is **secluded** is in a place by itself.

secure (sih-KYAWR) safe from risk or danger. To **secure** is to get; to fasten.

shelter (SHEHL-tuhr) a place that provides protection

sincere (sihn-SIHR) honest or genuine

somber (SAHM-buhr) serious or gloomy

standard (STAN-duhrd) common or usual. **Standardized** (STAN-duhr-dyzd) means common or usual.

status (STAY-tuhs) the condition of something or where it stands

stellar (STEH-luhr) outstanding

strategy (STRA-tuh-jee) a careful plan for getting something done

submit (suhb-MIHT) to give in or to give something over to someone else

succession (suhk-SEH-shuhn) a group of people or things that comes or happens one after the other

suitably (SOO-tuh-blee) in a proper or right way

surplus (SEHR-pluhs) more than what you need

T

taper (TAY-puhr) to become gradually narrower toward one end or to gradually lessen

technique (tehk-NEEK) a method or way of doing something

technology (tehk-NAH-luh-jee) the systematic use of science to solve problems. People often think of electronic products, like computers, as **technology**.

temporary (TEHM-puh-rer-ee) for a short time

theorize (THEE-uh-ryz) to make a guess based on facts. A **theory** (THEE-uh-ree) is an idea based on facts. **Theoretical** (thee-uh-REH-tih-kuhl) describes something that is based on facts but is not proven.

tire (TYR) a band of rubber around the edge of a wheel

tiring (TYR-ihng) causing fatigue or weariness. To **tire** means to feel in need of rest or sleep.

toiling (TOYL-ihng) doing very hard, usually physical, work

topple (TAH-puhl) to fall over or to fall down

torrential (taw-REHNT-shuhl) describes a rushing flow of water

trait (TRAYT) a special quality or characteristic that describes someone

transport (trants-PAWRT) to move something from one place to another. **Transportation** (trants-pawr-TAY-shuhn) is what is used to move things from place to place. A **transporter** (trants-PAWR-tuhr) moves things from place to place.

turmoil (TUHR-moyuhl) great confusion

U

unaware (uhn-uh-WEHR) not knowing about something

undergo (uhn-duhr-GOH) to experience something that you would usually rather not experience

undoutbedly (uhn-DAW-tuhd-lee) certainly, surely, or without a doubt

unfit (uhn-FIHT) in poor shape or condition to do something

unlimited (uhn-LIH-muh-tuhd) has no end

unrelated (uhn-rih-LAY-tuhd) not connected

V

vendor (VEHN-duhr) someone who sells something. To **vend** (VEHND) is to sell something.

version (VUHR-zhuhn) an account of an event or one side of things

vicinity (vuh-SIH-nuh-tee) an area around something

vivid (VIH-vuhd) bright, strong, and clear

voluntarily (VAH-luhn-ter-ih-lee) freely choosing to do something

W

whereas (hwer-AZ) on the other hand or in contrast to

withstand (wihth-STAND) to stand up to or to resist successfully

worthwhile (wuhrth-HWYUHL) worth your time, effort, or attention

Y

yield (YEELD) to give up or to produce